FUTURE PROSPECTS OF SERVICE TAX

FUTURE PROSPECTS OF SERVICE TAX

By

Dr. Yogita Beri

Assistant Professor

Department of Economics

Vasanta College for Women

Rajghat Fort (BHU) Varanasi

(INDIA)

DISCOVERY PUBLISHING HOUSE PVT. LTD.

NEW DELHI-110 002

Published by:

Tilak Wasan

DISCOVERY PUBLISHING HOUSE PVT. LTD.

4383/4B, Ansari Road, Darya Ganj
New Delhi-110 002 (India)
Phone : +91-11-23279245, 43596064-65
Fax : +91-11-23253475
E-mail : parul.wasan@gmail.com
discoverypublishinghouse@gmail.com
web : www.discoverypublishinggroup.com

***First Edition:* 2012**

ISBN: 978-93-5056-084-6

Future Prospects of Service Tax

Printed at:
Shree Balaji Art Press
Delhi

Preface

Service rendered as the basis for levying taxes could be traced through ancient *Hindu* scriptures. The *Dharmasastra's* clearly depicted that the taxes were considered as the wages of king or his reward for protecting his subjects. Service Tax in modern times is a new phenomenon and presently levied in more than 150 countries. Service Tax is of the nature of consumption tax. Consumerism and consumption tax must grow together in the era of Liberalization, Privatization and Globalization. Contribution of service sector as a percentage of GDP has already reached to a substantially high level in developed countries. Such a ratio is gradually improving in developing countries. In India this ratio reached at the level of 50 per cent with the turn of the century and presently is more than 55 per cent of the GDP. Visualizing the rate of growth of service sector several countries have beneficially utilized the Service Tax as an instrument for raising revenue.

In India Service Tax was adopted in the year 1994-95. Initially it was levied upon three selected services *viz.* stock broker services, general insurance and telephone. Its scope is continuously expanding and presently 110 services are subjected to Service Tax. The experience of last one and half decade shows a great potential in Service Tax. Since last 5 year's government is trying its best to move towards a comprehensive Goods and Services Tax (GST). It will be a landmark in the process of indirect taxes reform in the country. The new system of GST is proposed to be implemented from 1st April 2010.

The present study has been taken up to clearly examine the concept of Service Tax in its historical perspective and to analyze various issues relating to this tax in the context of the existing tax structure in India. The constitutional and other legal constraints in the context of the Indian Federal Structure in implementation of the GST are also analyzed.

Author

Acknowledgements

Any accomplishment requires the efforts of many people and this work is not different in this respect. I am extremely grateful to my supervisor Prof.Kiran Barman, Head, Department of Economics, for suggesting a lively subject for this project and for her valuable, persistent and selfless guidance to me. Her guidance goes beyond the conventional boundaries of supervision. Her meticulous efforts, motivation and constant interest in my research work have facilitated me to conduct the research work in an uninterrupted and timely manner. I also take this opportunity to thank Prof.A.K.Jain, Dean, Faculty of Social Sciences, Banaras Hindu University for his advice and encouragement.

I want to extend my sincere thanks to Prof. Inu Mehta and Prof. A.K.Gaur of the Department of Economics for helping me in data analysis and for the support and cooperation they have provided me in the calculation of buoyancy of the Service Tax.

I want to express my deep regards and gratitude to Prof. S.K.Verma (Retd.) Law School, Banaras Hindu University who has been very kind, helpful and supportive to me throughout my research work. I express my deep gratitude to him for being a source of inspiration for me. I am also thankful to Mr.M.M.Parekh a leading tax advocate of Varanasi for providing me with rich material on the topic of my research and for moral support.

I would like to record my special thanks to all my respected teachers in the Department of Economics and all the staff members of the Central Library and the departmental Libraries of various sister faculties of Banaras Hindu University, Varanasi; National Institute of Public Finance and Policy, New Delhi; Indian Institute Of Public Administration, New Delhi; Ratan Tata Library, Delhi School of Economics, New Delhi; National Council of Applied Economic Research, New Delhi; Jawaharlal Nehru University, New Delhi; Indian institute of Foreign Trade, New Delhi; for so kindly extending me all reference facilities at their end.

No words can express my feelings for my parents. I have been able to complete this work because of the endless love, patience and sacrifices made by my parents. I want to express my sense of affection and appreciation for my sister Ms. Udita Beri and brother Amulya Beri for their constant help. I also owe a lot of cooperation extended by my friends. Last but not the least I must mention that I am solely responsible for any mistake, if any, which might have been overlooked in my work.

Yogita Beri

Contents

Principles of Taxation and Historical Perspectives

THE PERSPECTIVE

Finance is the pivot around which all activities of an organized political group move. Public revenue forms the life blood of any form of Government. The very foundation of all political institutions is public revenue. Public finance is the science as well as an art to manage the income and expenditure of each and every society. One of the legitimately expected functions of public finance is to accept the challenging task of economic reconstruction and establish a just social order. In ancient time the task of pooling the resources for the welfare of the community was simple as their wants were limited. In present time the task of government to collect public revenue is tremendous in view of the ever growing functions of the government and the needs of the society. In modern times 'economic development' is the phrase used as a standard to indentify the stage of progress or status of any country throughout the world.

Economic development is a multifarious socio-economic process. It aims not only economic growth in the sense of an increase in the GDP or the per capita income or consumption level but implies an overall development of the community. An efficient distribution of the increased production is equally necessary so as to ensure that fruits of progress reach to the common man and the object of socio-economic justice be achieved. To promote the simultaneous achievement of steady growth and a high level of employment, avoidance of inflation and unequal distribution of income and wealth, maintaining the foreign trade equilibrium and the stable currency, development of technical know–how and the requisite infrastructure, elimination of mass-poverty, hunger, illiteracy and diseases are *inter-alia*, some of the basic objectives to be achieved.

A primary and traditional function of taxation is mobilization of resources for the ever expanding financial needs of the state. The policy for resource mobilization is primarily directed towards most efficient use of the available resources, proper and effective allocation of the unutilized resources and tapping of new sources. Taxation has become one of the most important instruments of economic development. It is the weapon through which the state can achieve different objectives *e.g.* reduction in the concentration of wealth in fewer hands and restrict the use of money for the detriment of the community at large. Government can implement its ambitious development scheme through taxation measures. It can regulate expenditure, give a direction to consumption, encourage foreign trade and achieve self-sufficiency through taxation[1]. The function of any efficient tax system is to raise revenue in a just and equitable manner.

The classical economists have classified the taxes into two categories: direct and indirect on the basis of their incidence. In case of direct tax the burden rest upon the person who pays as well as bear its impact, on the other hand when the incidence is passed on to others it is said to be indirect tax. In India, instrument of taxation has been used to accomplish various objectives such as restraining or curtailing consumption and transferring resources from consumption to investment, enlarging the area of incentives to save and invest, transferring resources from the hands of the general people to those of the government machinery to make public investment and reducing economic inequalities. It may, however be emphasized here that co-ordination amongst the various objectives is desirable and in a situation if any conflict arises the state must identify clearly the priorities in terms of the objectives to be achieved. Such an approach will ensure efficiency of the instrument of taxation. Further the tax structure must keep on changing with the changing needs of the economy. A tax policy is only a means to an end. Therefore the socio-economic goals must be well determined and the policy measures are to be moulded to achieve these objectives.

In India with the starting of first Five Year Plan the initiative was taken for economic reforms since 1952. The Indian economy was suffering from low level of infrastructure and extremely low level of capital investment. The process of industrialization was at a very low level and therefore India adopted the structure of mixed economy with a gradual development of public sector undertakings. The incentives were given its free hands but in spite of their liberal use they were not of much help in encouraging the infusion of foreign investment and technological knowledge to boost the Indian economy. The picture remained the same till 1990. During early four decades of planning, efforts were primarily directed towards rapid industrialization and accelerated rate of economic growth. However the experience was just reverse. The worst phase reached when there was acute shortage of foreign exchange and the country faced crisis in balance of payment, the exports were stagnating and imports were rising.

The economy took a U-turn in 1991 and the policy of Liberalization, Privatization and Globalization (LPG) was introduced. This step is being treated as gateway to export-led growth for the Twenty-first Century. Under this policy, several steps were taken for tax reform as well. Though the primary function of the tax system remained to raise revenue it has to be in an efficient and equitable manner to maintain the liquidity in the market. Due to the effect of globalization there started a flood of foreign capital resulting into rapid industrialization. However there was more and more demand for government expenditure for strengthen the infrastructure sector and welfare activities which necessitated the acceleration in the process of tax reform. The trend was started to dismantle public sector and diverting the government resources towards developing infrastructure at a faster rate. Comprehensive tax reform had to be an essential element of any programme of stabilization of economy and its structural reforms. Macro-economic stabilization requires reduction in fiscal deficit which had to depend more on high tax collection. Accordingly, the policy of comprehensive reform of direct and indirect taxation was also undertaken. With an ever expanding growth of market economy great philip has been given to consumerism. Consumerism and consumption tax (including service tax) must grow together. It has spread throughout the country. It is a great opportunity for widening the tax base. The enormous increase in the production of goods and services both quantitative and qualitative has opened new fields for taxing services along with tax on goods.

Services are very important part of our international trade as well. For the first time World Trade Organization (WTO) accepted the significance of trade related services along with trading in industrial and agricultural produce. This sector contributes around 55 per cent to the Gross Domestic Product (GDP). Therefore, it is justified to tax on services along with goods and treat both of them alike. Service tax was introduced in India for the first time in the year 1994-95 through the Finance Act, 1994. Chapter V of the Finance Act deals with the imposition of Service Tax. To begin with it was levied only on three services *viz.* telephone, general insurance and stock broker's services. Thereafter scope of service tax has been continuously widening every year and a good number of services were brought under the Service Tax net. Presently the list includes 110 taxable services. Initially the tax was levied at the rate of five per cent which has gradually been increased to 12.36 per cent and though now reduced to 10 per cent. Presently the effective rate is 10.30 per cent (including education cess).

The revenue collection from Service Tax also shows steady rise since its inception in the year 1994-95. It shot up from a meager figure of Rs.410 crores in 1994-95 to a gigantic figure of Rs.51,301 crores in 2007-08. The revised estimate for the year 2008-09 is Rs. 65,000 crores and the Interim budget for the year 2009-10 is expected to touch Rs. 68,900 crores. Through the help of a modernized and efficient administration and appropriate tax reform, the revenue earning from service sector is expected to rise further in a geometric proportion.

While recognizing the potential of Service Tax there are few points worth mentioning there are certain inherent bottlenecks which are being faced in expanding the scope of service tax. Services unlike goods do not have any physical form. It is a complex task to comprehend various activities which come under a particular taxable service.

The Service Tax is envisaged as the tax of the Twenty-first Century. The inclusion of all value added services in the tax net with a few necessary and appropriate exemptions would certainly yield a larger amount of revenue and make the existing tax structure more elastic. The final destination of the reform process would be the introduction of a comprehensive Goods and Service Tax (GST) through merging excise duty, Value Added Tax (VAT), Central Sales Tax (CST) and Service Tax into it. The Finance Minister has announced that GST would be introduced by 2010. In view of the adoption of a Federal Government structure, where powers of taxation are shared between the Central and the State it is proposed that India would have to adopt a dual GST system.

TAX PLANNING, TAX AVOIDANCE, TAX EVASION AND BLACK MONEY: A CONCEPTUAL ANALYSIS

The dividing line between tax planning, tax avoidance and tax evasion is very thin.

Tax Planning

Planning is today indispensable. It involves deciding in the present, what is to be done in future, how it is to be done and timing thereof. Tax Planning is resorted to by the tax payers with a view to minimizing the outflow on account of tax. The assessees have realized today that with the increasing burden of direct and indirect taxes, they have no choice but to plan their tax payments. Tax Planning is defined as "Avoidance of tax liability by so arranging the commercial affairs that charge of tax is mitigated." Tax Planning is adoption of such scheme whereby the taxpayer makes use of all concessions, reliefs, rebates and exemptions available to him under various tax legislations and pays the minimum possible tax. It implies full compliance of all tax laws and meeting the tax obligations. It is a legal measure.

> "Tax Panning is legitimate provided it is within the framework of law. Colourable devices cannot be part of tax planning and it is wrong to encourage or entertain the belief that it is honourable to avoid the payment of tax by resorting to dubious methods."[2]

The basic objectives of tax planning are: reduction of tax liability, minimization of litigation, productive investment, healthy growth of economy and economic stability.

Tax Avoidance

It is an exercise where the assessee tries to take advantage of the loopholes of law and by-passes the tax liability. With all this he remains outside the purview of law. Without resorting to illegal means one effects a reduction in one's tax liability. There is an element of malafide motive involved in tax avoidance. Any planning of tax which though done strictly according to legal requirement but defeats the basic intention of legislature behind the statute can be termed as instance of tax avoidance. Though earlier tax avoidance was considered completely legitimate, at present it is not so. Tax Avoidance is 'the art of dodging tax without breaking the law.'

Tax Evasion

All methods by which tax liability is illegally avoided are termed as tax evasion. An assessee guilty of tax evasion may be punished under the relevant laws. Tax evasion involves stating an untrue statement knowingly, submitting misleading documents, suppression of facts, not maintaining proper accounts of income earned, omission of material facts at the time of assessment *etc.*. Tax evasion is thus, a deliberate manipulation of facts. It is an economic and social crime. Main evil of tax evasion is proliferation of black money which is the root cause of curbing the achievement of socio-economic goals of planned development.

Black Money

Black Money is the money acquired through illegal means and not accounted for. It is an elusive term and yet to be defined precisely. It is *tainted money* that is not clean and has a stigma attached to it. The term *Black Market* and *Black Money* came into vogue during the Second World War. It originates in clandestine transactions but remains in circulation. In due course of time, it took the enormous shape to a *Parallel Economy.*

The problem of black money is in the forefront in the field of taxation right from the early fifties in India.[3] About four decades ago it was rightly pointed out:

> "In recent years, the extent of black money and tax evasion has assumed such dimension that no section of the community seems to be quite immune from their virulent grip."[4]

It astonishes to find that even enlightened classes like the members of legal profession are not free from this evil. To quote M.C.Setalvad:

> "Standards of professional conduct have woefully fallen and tax evasion is freely practiced by prominent seniors."[5]

Undoubtedly a number of transactions related to taxable services are not accounted for inspite of several stringent penalties. It is a tremendous task to bring such transactions into the Service Tax net.

Principles of Taxation

The principles of taxation are as old as the history of taxation. The Indian Classical thinkers laid down various provisions for tax levied. According to them taxes should be levied in accordance with the provision of *Shastra* and it should not be burdensome upon the taxpayers.

In his monumental work 'History of *Dharmasastra*', the chapter dealing with *Kosa* (Treasury or Finance) P.V.Kane remarks:

> "The first principle was that the king could not levy, according to the *smrtis,* taxes at his pleasure or sweet will, that the rates of taxes which the King was entitled to levy were fixed by the *smrtis* and varied only according to the commodity and also according as the times were normal or there was danger of invasion or some other calamity impending."[6]

Not only this, further, father of Indian economics science, *Kautilya* has also presented valuable thoughts relating to the state financial management. K.V. Rangaswami Aiyangar[7] in his study states that all modern cannons of taxation were emerged from the ancient Indian (thoughts) history of Taxation. The *Kautilya's* advice that the State should imitate the wise gardener, who collects only the ripe fruits. In *Mahabharta* we can find that the State was enjoined to permit the resources of the subjects to grow before imposing taxes on them. A tax should be collected after a careful consideration of place *(desa)* and time *(kala)*. These involves 'canon of convenience'. *Kautilya* also state that the taxes should be paid in definite proportion and amount, as well as the time and manner of its payments, are to be as clear to the payer as to the tax collector, this is *canon of certainty*. The canon of economy and canon of equality are also described in ancient historical work. *Manusmriti* advocates that ability to pay should be considered an important aspect of the state financial management, particularly the tax management. *Kautilya* clarify that the tax administration should attempt to minimize the cost on tax administration.

In Modern times Adam Smith first systemized the rules that should govern a rational system of taxation. In *The Wealth of Nations*[8] he set down four general canons: that taxes should be based on the individual's ability to pay and that they should be certain, convenient and economical.

1. The subjects of every state ought to contribute towards the support of the government as nearly as possible, in proportion to their respectively abilities; that is, in proportion to the revenue which they respectively enjoy under the protection of the state...
2. The tax which each individual is bound to pay ought to be certain and not arbitrary. The time of payment, the manner of payment, the quantity to be paid, ought all to be clear and plain to the contributor and to every other person....
3. Every tax ought to be levied at the time or in the manner in which it is most likely to be convenient for the contributor to pay it....
4. Every tax ought to be so contrived as both to take out and keep out of the people as little as possible over and above what it brings into the public treasury of the state....[9]

Today only the first of these canons is considered of prime importance. The other three have been overshadowed by more recent development in the theory of taxation. Now-a-days the criteria of a good tax system are wide ranging and complex. Some of them fall under the heading of revenue productivity. In the modern welfare state taxes should be levied with the principle of universality, equality and responsive to the individual's ability to pay. The principle of universality postulates that all persons able to pay should be taxed uniformly, and that exemptions from any tax must serve overall economic, social, and other goals. The ability-to-pay principle requires that the total tax burden be distributed among individuals according to their capability to bear it, taking into account all of the relevant personal characteristics in such a way that the relative loss in economic capacity resulting from the tax is equal. The primary indicator of ability to pay is income, complemented by the subsidiary consideration of wealth. The equality principle requires that persons in the same or similar positions so far as tax purposes are concerned be subject to the same tax liability. In practice the equality principle is often disregarded both intentionally and un-intentionally. Taxation involves some type of compulsion. Therefore, the collection of taxes may have significant effects upon the behaviour of individuals. The functioning of the economy along with the behaviour of taxpayers must be taken into consideration in the selection of taxes if the tax structure is not to interfere with the attainment of the economic goals of the society. As the payment of taxes gives no direct benefit, it merely reduces the disposable income of the tax payers and imposes a sacrifice on them. It is therefore necessary that aggregate sacrifice for community as a whole should be minimized. The aggregate sacrifice of the community is minimized when the marginal sacrifice of an individual tax payer is equal or as nearly equal as possible.

However, there are difficulties in practice and violations of horizontal equity can be found throughout a tax code. It is almost universally accepted that the person who have greater ability should pay more to the government, than those who are relatively less well off. There are thus, certain basic objective standards used for the measurement of ability to pay taxes. These are income, value of property or wealth and finally consumption expenditure. Thus, the problem arises regarding the choice of tax base. Base of taxation is a legal description of the object with reference to which the tax applies.

HISTORICAL PERSPECTIVE OF TAXATION

The history of taxation is traced back to the progressive days of civilization. Taxes played a relatively minor role in ancient world.

In ancient Egypt land taxes were fixed liabilities regardless from the return of the land. The Inheritance and Capitation taxes were also levied. The tax collectors were known as *scribes*. Some of the Egyptian taxes were also followed in ancient Greece and Rome.

In Greece, direct taxes on income and wealth were unknown. Taxes were imposed on income from mines. They are also found in the form of tribute from subjugated country, gift from wealthy citizen and taxes on trade and consumption. Revenue was also collected through inheritance, capitation taxes and emergency levies. In Greece free citizens had different tax obligation from slaves.

In Rome, consumption taxes and custom duties were the primary source of government revenue. Taxes are also found of certain direct *Tributum* paid by citizen usually levied as a head tax. This tax was extended to real state holdings. In the time of Julius Caeser one per cent general sales tax was imposed. In Rome, initially the inheritance tax was five per cent later on change to 10 per cent. However, close relatives of deceased were exempted. In the early period the task of tax collection was left to middle man (Tax farmers) who contracted to collect the taxes for a share of the proceeds. During Ceaser's regime collection was delegated to civil servants. Direct taxes on income and wealth were unknown in ancient Egypt, Greece and Rome. An important land mark is found in the middle ages. When the ancient direct taxes were replaced by indirect taxes. The trend is well depicted as:

> "In the Middle Ages many of these ancient taxes, especially among the direct levies, vanished and gave way to a variety of obligatory services and a system of "aids"(most of which amounted to gifts). The main indirect taxes were transit duties and market fees. In the cities, the concept developed of a tax obligation encompassing all residents: the burden of taxes on certain foods and beverages was intended to be borne partly by consumer and partly by producers and tradesman."[10]

British tax system followed by the Roman system and land being the primary source of wealth, also became the primary source of taxation. Both local and Central government in England followed land taxes initially based on area and later on annual rental value. Growth of foreign and domestic commerce between 14th and 19th centuries made the way for import and export duties and internal excise. Rebellion against arbitrary and oppressive taxation played an important role in the history of taxation in many countries. It has been aptly remarked:

> "Such milestone in British constitutional history as Magna-Carta (1215) and The Bill of Right (1689) helped establish the principle of consent and representation in taxation. Failure to apply this principle to the colonies played no little part in American Revolution. Much of the desperation that exploded in The French Revolution grew out of France's tax system— one of the most oppressive and inequitable tax systems of all time. The French

> government as well as many other contractors known as tax farmers, who often employed harsh measures and arose the hatred of people. At the time of revolution the system was abolished and many of the tax farmers were executed."[11]

Further,

> "The development of tax law as a comprehensive general system is recent phenomenon. One reason for this is that no general system of taxation existed any country before the middle of the 19th century. In traditional essential aggregarian, societies, government revenues were drawn either from nontax sources (such as tribute. Income from royal domains and land rent) or, to a lesser extent from taxes on various objects (land taxes, tolls, customs and excises)."[12]

In 19th century, the gradual development of representative democratic government and as a result of industrial revolution, certain new forms of income and inheritance taxes were adopted and refined. The income taxation in modern times was introduced in 1789 by the younger Pitt as a temporary measure for meeting the increasing financial burden of Napoleon wars.[13] However it remained a temporary measure for raising revenue in war emergencies. In 1842, a peace time levy was made to help financial civil expenditure. By 1914, the personal income tax was adopted not one as important revenue instrument but also as an instrument for achieving socio-economic transformation in almost all the countries of the world.

TAXES IN ANCIENT INDIA

The tax system of ancient India is quite as complex as at present. The *Arthasastra* differentiate the forms of revenue not exactly according to their source but due to services rendered by king. Revenue was derived from land or from source other than land. Cesses were collected on the supply of water from State sources, the tree's tax on 1/6 of the tree's, medicinal herb, *etc.*, the profits of State mines and queries, the sale of forest produce and income from the royal herbs as well as the tax collected from owner's of private cattle farm. No attempt was made to distinguish between direct and indirect taxes. Similarly, rents, taxes, fees and royalty were also not differentiated further, no differentiation is found in tax and non-tax receipts. For ancient economist the only test of a tax was that it was due to the State. In ancient rules of taxation much importance was given to the fact that the tax when directly levied from the taxpayer there was the element of certainty in it. Land has been the mainstay of the State since ancient time. The rate varied from 1/6 to 1/12 of the produce. It varied according to the nature of the soil and the labour necessary to cultivate it. *Shukranitisara refers that:*

> "The rate be based on the amount of the produce, the cost of cultivation, the condition of the market, and the nature of the soil. The rate on barren and rocky land is not to exceed one-eighth, while it might be a fourth on rain-fed lands, a third on artificially irrigated lands, and as much as a half on lands which enjoyed continuous irrigation. The aim is always that, after the payment of the tax, a surplus should remain in the pocket of the cultivator. The net return to the cultivator should be double his outlay."[14]

TRACES OF SERVICE TAX IN ANCIENT INDIA

Service tax might be internationally recognized as a new levy and most promising revenue earner but in India it was always there right from vedic period. In Hindu scriptures king was authorized to levy and collect all kind of taxes as his wages (vetanena). In the *Shantiparva* of Mahabharata it is mentioned that:

> "The one-sixth Bali tax, import and export duties, fines and forfeitures collected from offenders—gathered in accordance

with the *Sastras* (law and constitution), as your wages *(vetanena),* shall constitute your revenue.[15]

The arthsastra differentiated the forms of revenue not according to their source but on the basis of services rendered by the king for his subjects. In Sukranitisara it is prescribed that:

> "God has made the king though master in form, the servant of the people, getting his wages (sustenance) in taxes for the purpose of continuous protection and growth."[16]

TAXES DURING MUGHAL PERIOD

In Mughal period, Babur, who was the founder of Mughal rule in India, had not followed any tax policy. Plundering was the main source of his estate income. In the year 1528, he levied a tax on its *amirs* of 30 per cent of their salaries as he was in need of funds for war equipment and gunpowder for the operation of cannons. *Ain-i-Akbari*(the official chronicles of the reign of Emperor Akbar) compiled by *Abul Fazl*, one of Akbar's courtiers is the primary sources of historical record of taxation system during Mughal Period.

During Akbar's reign, land revenue was the most important source of government revenue. Besides there were also the provisions of gifts, import and export duties. In the large market cities, in the sea harbours and at the borders of the Empire, import and export duties of 2.5 per cent ad valorem were levied; later on

Aurangzeb doubled this percentage for Hindus who had to make use of Muslim friends to evade this taxation. Another important direct tax levied by Mughal rulers was *jizya* or *zazia.*

It was a capitation tax on non-Muslims for the military service which they were required for their protection. The tax was later abolished by Akbar himself, but it was reintroduced and vigorously enforced by Aurangzeb in 1679 in the form of an income tax. The tax policy of Mughal was primarily guided by the religious considerations. The religious motive is apparent from the fact that discriminatory taxes on Hindus were encouraging Hindus to convert to Islam. This is one of the important contributory factors to the decline of Mughal after the death of Aurangzeb in 1707.

TAXES DURING BRITISH RULE TO PRESENT PERIOD

In British India, the first board of revenue was setup in Calcutta in the year 1786 to regulate taxes on import and export. In the year 1808, a new board of trade was established under the Regulation IX of 1810 Articles liable to Custom duties were classified under 86 heads. In 1833, Tariff included as many as 235 specified articles. The uniform Tariff Act was introduced in 1859 throughout the British India. The general rate of duties was 10 per cent which was subsequently revised to 7 per cent in 1864. Textile products were the primary target for taxation. Beside custom and excise, town tax was applicable on certain goods produced ion British India. In 1878 the government passed the Sea Custom Act. The provision relating to sea, air and land customs were consolidated and the Custom Act, 1962 was enacted followed by Custom Tariff Act, 1975. The Indian Salt Act, 1882 was the first enactment to levy tax on manufacture of salt. Fine cotton yarn was subjected to excise duty in 1894 at the rate of 5 per cent *ad valorem* and extended to certain other items and clothes of other variety in 1896. Motor spirit was brought under the excise net in the year 1917 and kerosene in the year 1922. The year 1934 was the landmark in the history of excise taxation when excise duties were imposed in sugar, matches and steel ingots. The duties were imposed in tyres in 1941 and vegetable products, tobacco in the year 1943 to meet the Second World War finances. Coffee, tea and betel-nuts were brought under the net in 1944, Cigarettes in 1948 and mill-made cotton clothes in 1949. Till the year 1944, excise duties were levied under 16 separate Acts. All these enactments were consolidated into the Central Excise and Salt Act, 1944 and the Central Excise Rule, 1944.

Income tax was the first direct tax to be introduced in the year 1860. It was imposed on Ad-hoc basis to meet the heavy expenditure incurred to control the Indian mutiny of 1857. It was levied on a permanent basis in the year 1886. It was replaced by Indian Income Tax Act, 1918. In 1917, a new tax was introduced by Super-tax Act, 1917 which was subsequently replaced by the Super-tax Act, 1920. The Indian Income Tax Act, 1918 and Super-tax Act, 1920 were later consolidated into Indian Income Tax Act, 1922, which finally got repealed by the Income Tax Act, 1961. It is further proposed to be redrafted as the Act of 2010.

For the British Indian provinces, the chief source of income was land revenue followed by Provincial excise mainly on liquor and stamp duty. Although, under the Government of India Act, 1935, Provincial Government had been authorized to levy sales tax, it formed a very low component of their revenue till independence. The province of Bombay levied a tax on the sale of tobacco in 1938. A retail sales tax on motor spirit and lubricants was imposed by Central Provinces (now Madhya Pradesh) in the same year. A multi-point general sales tax was levied in Madras Province at the rate of half per cent in 1939 under the Madras General Sales Tax Act. In 1985, the tariff schedule was taken out from the Central Excise and Salt Act 1944 and the Central Excise Tariff Act, 1985 was enacted to consolidate the Tariff Schedule. The Custom Tariff Act was also enacted in 1985.

Service as a tax base has came to be adopted recently in various countries. In some countries it is integrated with VAT and in others with the system of sales tax. Service Tax was introduced in Malaysia in 1975, Singapore in 1994, New Zealand in 1986, Philippines in 1988, Canada in 1991, Australia in 2000. Goods and Services Tax was proposed as a Value Added Tax in Hongkong adopted and dropped in the same year during 2006. There was a fierce battle among local taxpayers, law makers, journalists, politicians and was ultimately dropped in the end of the year.

The report of the Tax Reform Committee 1991 under the Chairmanship of Dr. Raja J. Chelliah has laid down the blueprint for reforming the indirect tax system in India. Emphasizing the need for broadening the tax base which would make possible as lowering of rates, it was observed that:

> "In respect of indirect taxes, such broadening has to take the form of covering (*a*) almost all commodities other than raw products of agriculture (*b*) many, if not most, services and (*c*) all stages of production or transactions. This is accomplished under an ideal system of VAT."[17]

In 1994, the Government of India imposed tax on three selected services, the coverage of which is being extended from year to year. Service Tax today covers 110 services. A Value Added Tax called 'VAT' has taken the place of sales tax in most of the States and it is proposed that in April 2010 Goods and Services Tax (GST) will be introduced which would cover all major indirect taxes of Union and State Government.

REFERENCES

1. This modern function of taxation is well recognized by the Supreme Court of India in Elect Hotels and Investment Ltd. *vs.* Union of India, AIR 1990 SC 1664.
2. As per Rangnath Mishra J. in McDowell & Co. *vs.* C.T.O .(1985) 154 I.T.R. 148
3. The evidence is available to prove that the tendency towards tax evasion and avoidance existed even in ancient period.
4. Report of the Direct Taxes Enquiry Committee (Dec.1971, Ministry of Finance, Government of India) It was constituted on 2nd March 1970 under the Chairmanship of K.N. Wanchoo, Retd., Chief Justice of the Supreme Court of India.

5. Motilal C. Setalvad; My Life Law and Other Things, at 622.
6. Kane, P.V.(1946): History of Dharmasastra, Vol III, Bhandarkar Orient Research Institute, Poona;184-185
7. Aiyangar, K.V.(1965): Aspect of Ancient Indian Economic Thought, Banaras Hindu University:115-116
8. The Wealth of Nations; Book V, Chapter II.
9. The New Encyclopaedia Britannica(1985), Vol. 28, Encyclopaedia Britannica, Inc Chicago;410
10. New Encyclopaedia Britannica (1985), Vol. 28,Encyclopaedia Britannica, Inc, Chicago:409
11. The New Encyclopaedia Britannica (1969), Vol. 21, Encyclopaedia Britannica, Inc, Chocago:723-724
12. New Encyclopaedia Britannica (1985), Vol. 28,Encyclopaedia Britannica, Inc, Chicago:413
13. Holand, the most urbanized part Europe, levied its first income tax in 1797,Ostria in 1799, The Duchy of Baden in 1808 and Russia in 1812, the year Napoleon invaded it. As referred in Agrawal, Dr. Sanjeev Kumar(2006); Systematic Approach to Indirect Taxes, Bharat Law House Pvt. Ltd., New Delhi: 2
14. Aiyangar, K.V.(1965): Aspect of Ancient Indian Economic Thought, Banaras Hindu University:115-116
15. Jayaswal, K.P.(1967): Hindu Polity: A Constitutional History of India in Hindu Times(Parts I & II), The Banglore Printing and Publishing Co. Ltd.: 320
16. *Ibid* at 321
17. Report of the Tax Reform Committee (1991) constituted under the Chairmanship of Dr. Raja J. Chelliah, p. 122.

2

Review of Literature

The various available literature on different aspects of public finance especially taxation: direct, indirect and Service Tax depicts the increasing role of service sector in the Indian economy. After independence India initiated the economic development process through Five Year Plans. The prime objective of this process was to move India on the road of accelerated economic growth and development. The endeavour was to achieve century's growth within decades. For three decades the Indian economy could not grow more than five per cent[1]. For nearly five decades in spite of the best efforts Indian economy remained a slow developing economy indicating low income, low savings, low investment and high rates of taxation resulting into low rate of growth.

The economy took a U-turn since 1991 when India moved from a restricted economy towards a process of Globalization, Privatization and Liberalization. At this stage the importance of the potentiality of service sector was recognized at national and international level. India realized the truth behind the policy of low tax rates resulting into increase in revenue and throughout expansion of economy. For the first time L.K. Jha Committee on Indirect Taxes (1978) explored the possibility of raising revenue through introduction of Service Tax, but due to several reasons it was not considered practical to bring services into the tax net. Tax Reform Committee (1991) under the chairmanship of Dr. Raja J. Chelliah strongly recommended the need and justification for imposing tax on services. Consequently through the Finance Act, 1994. Tax on three important services *viz.* Telephone, Stock Broker and General Insurance were initiated. Gradually the Service Tax gained currency and expanded the tax base and presently comprehends 110 services.

The growing importance of service sector and the ever increasing role of Service Tax in revenue kitty attracted the attention of financial analysts and scholars. While analyzing the literature on Service Tax it is found that the most of the literature is informative in nature. This feature is natural due to short experience of fifteen years of the functioning of the tax. A brief review of certain important selected studies on various aspects of Service Tax is attempted in this chapter.

BOOKS

Lakdawala, D.T. (1956): *'Taxation and the Plan'*, (Popular Book Depot, Bombay-7)

This work on the relationship of taxation and planning has been divided in four chapters. First is in search of revenue, second for equality, third private sector, fourth development with stability. The work discussed Kaldor's report on Indian Tax Reform at great length. The first chapter describes elasticity of Tax system, recommendations of the Taxation Enquiry Commission and various taxation measures adopted for encouraging savings and investment. Second chapter deals with various aspects of equality such as economic development and equality, demand for gender equality, functional and non-functional inequalities *etc....*

Due, John F. (1970): *'Indirect Taxation in Developing Economics'*, (The John Hopkins Press, Baltimore and London).

The present work describes the role of indirect taxation in developing economies and deal with the changing dimensions and structure of indirect taxes. It also define the term indirect taxes, discusses advantages and disadvantages of indirect taxes, objectives to be considered in framing indirect tax structure *i.e.* optimal growth, optimal equity, optimal resource allocation, stabilization *etc.*. Beside these the study also deals with the problems of developing appropriate indirect tax system in developing economies. It also deals with potential effects of indirect taxation in economic development.

Prasad, Kunwar Deo (1987): 'Taxation in Ancient India', (Mittal Publications, Delhi).

The present work is an attempt to deal comprehensively with all the important aspects of taxation in India from the earliest times up to the Gupta Period. The author rightly states that taxation has been the main pillar of the financial structure of states from very ancient times as also in modern time. The book describes different taxes levied during this period. This present monograph aims at presenting a comparative study of the principles and tenets of ancient Indian tax system. The book also deals with different taxes such as Land cess, commercial taxes and also analyses the revenue administration of these taxes. This book also gives a survey of the conditions of contemporary history of Indian society.

Jha Raghbendra (1987): '*Modern Theory of Public Finance*', (Wiley Eastern Ltd.)

The book gives an overview on different theoretical aspects of public finance. It is mainly divided into four parts: (*i*) modern welfare economics; (*ii*) economies of taxation; (*iii*) applied welfare problems; and (*iv*) Indian Public Finance. The last section of this book has three chapters. The first chapter gives an overview of the Indian public sector, second chapter reviews the tax structure of the India economy and last chapter reviews some problems of centre-state financial relations.

Jain, Inu. (1988): '*Resource Mobilization and Fiscal Policy in India*', (Deep & Deep Publication, New Delhi)

The present study examines in detail the relative importance and the role of various fiscal instruments, like taxation, public borrowing, surpluses of public enterprise and deficit financing in raising revenue. It also examines in detail the individual components in the tax structure of the Union and State Governments. A special feature of the study is that it includes the responsiveness of the aggregate Union and State taxes and selected individual taxes to change in national income. The author has also given important suggestions to widen the tax base, make it more productive and revenue elastic and simpler to understand and administer. The emergent problem of increasing burden of servicing India's ever growing debt and avoiding its moving towards a situation of 'debt trap' has also been discussed in the study.

Jha S.M. (1990): '*Taxation and the Indian Economy*', (Deep & Deep Publications, New Delhi)

The present book makes a modest attempt to examine the contribution of taxation to the transformation of national economy. The study quantifies the instrumentality of taxation in the process of resource mobilization, capital formation, product and productivity acceleration, national income generation and economic transformation. The acceleration of production and productivity helps raising the standard of living of masses, makes possible generation of demand, vitalizes the income re-distribution programme and sub serves socio-economic interest. Resources generate resources. This principle is based on in based on the monetary principle that money begets money. If in the economic reservoir, we have limited resources, it becomes difficult to generate and mobilize them in the best interest of national economy or to the best advantages of society. Here, taxation acts as an atom. It augments revenue of the government and reserves elbow room for the mobilization of resources which open doors for formation of capital, development of the national economy, well being of the masses and so on.

Kaur, Harjeet (1990): '*Taxation and Development Finance in India*', (Classical Publishing Company, New Delhi)

This book is essentially a fiscal exercise in economic development. In the developing economy taxation plays an increasingly important role as an instrument of development and the elasticity and buoyancy of the structure have been quantitatively measured in term of statistical techniques. The basic objective of this book is to test empirically the hypothesis in the Indian context.

Mukerjee, Suman K.(1994): '*Textbook of Economic Development*', (Orient Longman).

This book on economic development is divided into four parts. The first three parts deals with development theories, strategies and international trade and economic development. Part four is concerned with the problems and sources of financing economic development. The work also attempts to highlight the cross-currents of various aspects involved and the interdisciplinary nature of the problem of developing economies. It deals with the several issues of taxation such as role of direct and indirect taxes in India, deficit financing, fiscal policy in developing countries, role of indirect taxes in India. Being developing economy indirect taxes is the major portion of tax revenue in India and is generated primarily by way of excise and customs duties. The work also analyzes the various measures adopted towards indirect tax reforms.

Devereux, Michael P. (1996): '*The Economic of Tax Policy*', (Oxford University Press)

Taxes play a crucial role in the economies of all developed countries and the design of tax policy has very important implications for economic behaviour and welfare. This study provides an introduction to the important economic issues such as effect of tax policies on savings, investment, employment and its implication for international trade and investment *etc.*. This book is the collection of surveys on tax policy conducted by an international group of authors well known in the fields of public economics and taxation. Each chapter introduces a particular topic, presents the economic analysis in theoretical terms and then summarizes and discusses the most important current policy-issues applicable to all economies in general.

Chanda, Rupa (2002): '*Globalization of Services India's Opportunities and Constraints*', (Oxford University Press).

The service sector today encompasses a wide range of activities. It extends beyond the traditional areas of finance, insurance, transport, communication and tourism to new and dynamic ones such as software, electronic commerce, environment and educational services. This book assesses the implication of liberalization of multilateral trade and services in India. It provides a comprehensive account of the country's tradable service sector, its potential and problems in the context of the on-going WTO rounds of service negotiations. The book also presents an overview of trends in related services trade in the world economy it evaluates India's strength and weaknesses in this context and brings forth a comparative assessment of the extent of liberalization across the country's major trading partner. It also predicts policy implications for future trade prospects. It also evaluates liberalization strategies required to address cross-sectoral and multilateral issues. The book provides invaluable insight to policy-makers, business-persons and trade policy practitioners and negotiators. It will also appeal to academics and the wider public interested in the WTO negotiations trade in services.

Marwah, N. & Pahwa, S.K. (2002): '*Service Tax: Law and Procedures*', (New Age International Publishers, New Delhi).

The study deals Service Tax in a comprehensive manner. For this purpose the study is divided into four sections. Part *A* deals with each and every provision of Chapter V of the Finance Act, 1994, Service Tax Rule 1994, Service Tax Credit Rule 2002 and Forms to be used for Service Tax. Part *B* consists different taxable services in detail. Part *C* deals with Allied Acts as applicable to Service Tax. Part *D* consists of each and every exemption, notification related to Service Tax upto the year 2002. Besides these main parts there are various sub-parts also which deals with changes that have been brought under the Service Tax in the year 2002 like introduction of new services under the tax net, expansion of the existing services and other provision of the Act. It emphasized that services are increasingly gaining importance in Indian economy as well as give boost to tax revenue and its importance cannot be undermined any more.

Rustagi, T.R.(2002): '*Service Tax in India: Law and Practice*', (Deeparchie Publication)

The book covers comprehensively different aspects of Service Tax. It gives a detailed account of the history and introduction of Service Tax in India. The Service Tax Law in India owes its origin to chapter V of the Finance Act, 1994. It incorporates several amendments in the Service Tax provisions till the year 2002. The book contains a lucid description of all these changes for ease of reference to taxpayers, departmental officers, advocates and consultants. A special chapter on disputes and litigation describes how the law, procedure and implementation of Service Tax have stood the test of legal scrutiny. Special emphasis has been laid on explaining the legal provisions with regard to different services. Procedures have been covered in a suitable manner especially to cater the needs of various assesses liable to Service Tax.

Lavi, R. Mohan and Varadarajan, D. (2002): '*Service Tax: Concept, Practice and Procedure*', (Bharat Law House Pvt. Ltd, New Delhi).

The present study explains different problems relating to Service Tax with their solutions. Besides this it also explain the procedure of electronic Service Tax administration. Service-wise revenue trends in our country are also evaluated in it. This study emphasized that one of the objectives of taxation is growth with justice. Service Tax made its debut in India in 1994. This study aptly state the fact that bringing services under taxation is not simple as the services are provided by large groups of organized as well as unorganized service providers, including a large number of retailers who are scattered across the country. There are several services, which are of intermediate nature which create their own problems. The low level of education of service providers will also pose difficulties to both tax administration and assesses. Besides these there are also lots of problems and difficulties in the administration of tax that has been discussed in the study.

Reports on India's Tax Reforms, Academic Foundation, New Delhi (2003).

The present book includes a number of reports and papers on Tax Reforms such as Report of the Task force on Indirect taxes, Report of the Advisory Group on Tax Reforms 2001, The Chellaiah Committee Report 1992 and 1993 *etc*.. This book summarizes the fact that the process of fiscal reform was initiated along with the programme of liberalization in 1991. A Committee on India's Tax Reforms was set up under the Chairmanship of Raja J. Chellaiah. The Committee submitted its reports in 1992 and 1993 and made some bold recommendations. In July 2000, the Planning Commission set up on Advisory Group under the chairmanship of Parthasarathy shown to study Tax Policy and Tax Administration. On September 3, 2002 the Ministry of Finance and Company Affairs set up a Task Force on Indirect Taxes with the objective of bringing the indirect tax system and procedures at par with the best international practices.

Parthasathy, C. and Agarwal, Sanjiv(2004): '*A Handbook of Service Tax: Law, Practice and Procedure*', (Snow White Publication Pvt. Ltd., Mumbai)

This study covered the importance of service sector; need for Service Tax its future prospect. It also covered various other problems which had arisen in the course of the administration of service tax. Several suggestions were also given to widen the tax base and for making it more productive and revenue elastic as well as simpler to understand and administer. The study also contains statutory provisions of Service Tax, Service Tax Rules, Service Tax Credit Rules, and Applicability of provision of other Acts applicable to Service Tax such as Securities Contracts Rules 1957, Customs Act 1938, Sale of Goods Act 1930, Insurance Act 1938, Motor Vehicle Act 1888, Transfer of Property Act 1882 *etc.*.

Holani, Ravi (2005): '*Service Tax: An Indepth Analysis and Scope*', (Prakash Publications).

The present study on service tax deals with its different aspects. This work on service tax also describes the scope of tax, procedural provisions tax such as registration, payment of tax, books and records, filing of returns, assessment, appeals, demand and refunds, rectification of mistake, power of search, penalty, imposition of interest, revision *etc.*. Besides these it also deals with exemptions from the levy of Service Tax, advance rulings of the tax, exemption scheme for small service provider *etc.*. It observed that Service Tax is to be paid on all the services notified by the Government of India for the said purpose unless otherwise exempted. The said tax is on the service either provided by the specified category of service provider or provided at specified place.

Krishna, V.S. (2006): '*Indirect Tax Reforms: Challenge and Response*', (Abhinav Publications, New Delhi)

The present book seeks to examine the reference in three individual segments of indirect taxation—Central Excise, Customs and Service Tax. These together constitute 60 per cent of the total tax revenue in the country. While all the three taxes are indirect taxes, the dynamic of reforms in each of these individual segments has been different. The book seeks to examine tax reforms in each. These reforms have influenced the fortunes of a large number of manufacturing sectors. However, in respect of two—petroleum and textile—the influence has been significant. In two separate chapters, the past impact, the present changes and future course of action have been outlined. The book also has separate chapters on Central VAT and the proposed state VAT. Structurally it is divided into two parts. Part I deals with the post and present reform measure, while Part II examines the future course of indirect tax reforms. It also argues that tax reform is a 'Work-in Progress'. Expansion of tax base is an important theme in all the chapters. One immediate fallout of the tax reforms in India has been the declining tax to GDP ratio, but this may improve with policy initiatives to wider the tax base especially through Service Tax, phasing away of indirect tax exemptions and nationwide implementation of state VAT. The book also looks at the indirect tax administration. This study emphasizes designing of a modern tax administration with a view to make the system more assesses friendly and revenue efficient. By laying out a road map for the future, it offers useful suggestions for indirect tax reforms to the policy makers.

Gabhawala, Sunil B. (2006): '*Treatise on Service Tax: Law,Practice and Procedure*', (Bharat Law House Pvt.Ltd., New Delhi).

The present work is one of the most important study on Service Tax and it mainly emphasizes on the administrative aspect of Service Tax, classification of services, WTO classification of services, scheme of Service Tax laws, nature and scope of levy of the tax, CENVAT credit, *etc.* are discussed in the first part of the book. Part II of the study deals with the taxable services separately. This work finds that the share of service sector in the Indian economy has increased significantly over the years. The growth of any economy is evidenced by the vibrant growth of its service sector. The growing importance of service sector is an indicator of economic development of a country. Therefore, it is important to levy the tax on both goods and services.

Sury, M.M. (ed.) (2006): '*Taxation in India 1925 to 2007: History, Policies, Trends and Outlooks*', (New Century Publication, New Delhi)

The present book provides an exhaustive and critical account of the various aspects of the Indian tax system. It places current development in the fields of taxation in perspective.

Part I of the work traces the structural evaluation. It explains the legal framework and describes the present system of taxation in India quite elaborately. Besides being the main source of revenue, both for the Central and State Governments, taxation is an effective instrument to realize various socio-economic objectives of national policies.

Part II of the study reproduces edited extracts from the several reports on taxation published by the Government of India during 1925 to 2006. Recommendation of the various Commissions/ Working Groups on taxation set up by the Government constitute the core of tax policies followed in India during last 80 years. Taxation reports included in this book highlight contemporary issues in India's public finances and record measures suggested by experts from time to time to ensure soundness of public exchequer. These reports are an authentic and reliable source for the study of economic history of India.

Part III contains time series data (1950-51 to 2004-05) on tax revenues of Central and State Governments in India. It would be useful for a cross-section of academic community and researchers, both in India and abroad.

Part IV consists of three Appendices which provide supplementary information related to taxation in India. Part V contains glossary of taxation terms.

Datey, V.S. (2007) : '*Indirect Taxes: Law and Practice*', (Taxmann Publications Pvt. Ltd., New Delhi).

The book describe in detail various indirect taxes such as Central Excise, Custom Law, Service Tax and Central Sales Tax *etc.*. For this purpose it's divided in five parts. The third part of the book deals with the Service Tax and consist various chapters. These chapters deals with Background of Service Tax, Nature of Service Tax, Value of Taxable services, Procedure of Service Tax, Assessment of tax, Rectification of mistake and revision, Amount collected from tax, Penalties, Appeals, Export and Import of services.

Kumar, Dr. Sanjeev(2007): '*Systematic Approach to Indirect Taxes(with practical problems and solutions)*', (Bharat Law House Pvt. Ltd., New Delhi).

This study emphasizes the fact that indirect taxes play very important role in the revenue of Central Government. Indirect taxes are those taxes, which are paid by the taxpayers indirectly, when purchasing some goods or commodity or when hiring some services, which are taxable. These taxes are though borne by the taxpayers, but not paid by them directly to the Government. It elaborately deals with Excise Duty, Customs Duty, Sales Tax and Service Tax. Fifth part deal with different aspects related to Service Tax such as introduction to Service Tax Law, Definitions and concepts of various services, Liability of Tax, Payment and recovery, Advance Ruling, registration requirements and procedure, Assessments, Revision and Appeals, Records and Returns, offence and penalties *etc.*.

Gupta, S.S.(2008) : '*Taxman's Service Tax: How to Meet Your Obligations*", Vol. I and II, (Taxman Publication Pvt. Ltd.).

This work on Service Tax has been divided into two volumes and provides useful information on various aspects of Service Tax in India. The first volume describes basic propositions, exemptions, export and import of services, valuation of various taxable services. It also deals with various services in detail such as advertising agency's services, outdoor services *etc*.. Volume II describes the various other taxable services such as packaging activity services, work contract services *etc*.. It also analyze certain other aspects such as registration, payment, returns, Cenvat credit *etc*..

Sarangi, Gopinath(2008-09): '*Service Tax Manual*', (Centax Publications Pvt. Ltd., New Delhi).

In this study an attempt has been made to introduce the law relating to Service Tax to a layman. It explains the law and procedure governing service tax to make it a comprehensive book of reference. There is in-depth analysis of each taxable service including reference to important clarifications issued by Government, relevant provisions of Central Acts having a bearing on service tax law, exemption notifications, tabular charts, appendices *etc*.. The book also contains the details of new services and other legislative changes proposed to be made by the Finance Bill, 2008 along with the Budget 2008-09. This book emphasiszed the truth that Service Tax is the emerging field of taxation for raising Government revenue. When the Service Tax is integrated with the taxes on goods, it will lead to Value Added Tax. As the days pass by, whether there is single tax on goods and services or not, more services are to be brought under the service tax net. It would, therefore be useful for every person, concerned with tax on services to acquaint with tax liability, scope of levy, taxable event, value of taxable service, book-keeping, levy, collection and payment, consequences for non-compliance *etc.*, to be equipped with intricacies governing service tax law.

ARTICLES

Srivastava B.P.(1995): 'Service Tax—A Right step to broaden the tax base', *Excise Law Times*, Vol.78; A41-A43.

The present study describes the imposition of Service Tax as a process to broaden the tax base. The article describes the procedure and administration of Service Tax in India. It was imposed through the Finance Act 1994. It also describes the registration process, interest on late payment of the tax, penalty for failure to furnish return, collection and payment of Service Tax. The study also deals with punishment, failure and imprisoned related to Service Tax. It emphasizes that the share of service sector in GDP is increasing very fast and has been showing strong growth.

Rustagi T.R.(1998): 'Indirect Tax Reforms in Indian Economy', *Vikalpa*, Vol.23(1); 47-59.

This paper mainly emphasizes upon role, importance and reforms in the indirect taxes and also describes the evolution of indirect taxes in India and gives a brief outline of the system of indirect taxation in ancient India. This study confirms that the indirect tax structure of our country becomes more complex through various notifications, rates and exemptions. Government of India have set up several committees from time to time to examine the India's indirect tax structure in the past and made valuable recommendations. The present study mainly examines the recommendations of the Tax Reforms Committee 1991 headed by Dr. Raja J. Chelliah and also describes the reforms in Excise Duty, Custom Duty and Service Tax. The study points out that in stepping up the tax effort in India, indirect taxes have played an increasingly important role. They are called indirect taxes in the belief that they can be passed on to someone else while direct taxes are supposed to be borne by those on whom they are levied.

Katti, Prof. Vijaya(1998): 'Service Sector and Employment', *Yojana*, Vol.42(8),53-58.

The present study is mainly deals with the employment generation in service sector and it also compares the employment opportunities of different sectors such as industry, agriculture and service sector. The study also describes the growing importance of services in international trade. The study concludes that the most important services in international trade include transportation, travel, communication, media, business services, engineering and construction and banking and financial services. The study also shows that about 10 per cent of working population is employed in organized sector. About 55 per cent of the total employment in organized sector is concerned with service sector in both public and private sector. As far as private sector is concerned the share is smaller than the public sector.

Datey, V.S.(1998) : 'Service Tax: The Management Accountant', Vol. 33(12), 931-938.

The present paper covers various aspects of Service Tax in our country. The tax is administrated by Central Excise Department. The study covers following aspects of the tax-background of the Service Tax, taxable services, value of taxable service for charging Service Tax, basic exemption and few abatements, persons who bears expenses, no tax on services provided on sub-contract, tax payment only on actual amount received, exemption in respect of overseas projects, Service Tax on profession, engineering services, mandap keeper, company secretary's services, charted accountant services, manpower recruitment agency's services, procedure to be followed in payment of Service Tax *etc.*.

Bhowmik, Rita(2000) : 'Role of Service Sector in Indian Economy: An Input-Output Approach', *Artha Vijnana*, Vol.XLII(2), 158-169.

The objective of this paper is to study the rate of growth of service sector by identifying the service-intensive industries and its relation with the rest of the economy. To build a relation of service sector with the rest of the economy, the economy is divided into two separate blocks of industries— services and non services. An index is constructed to show the expansionary potential of the service sector on non-services sector. Empirical work is carried out with the input output data of India for the year 1991-92. The paper also describes different studies of social scientists of India like Mitra (1988), Datta (1989), Bhattacharaya and Mitra (1988) *etc.*.

Malegaon, Suresh S. (2001): 'The Liberalisation and Indirect Taxation: An X-ray', *Southern Economist*, Vol. 39, 9-12.

The purpose of the present paper is to evaluate the role of union indirect taxes on the process of liberalization, *i.e.* after 1991. It also examines the role of commodity taxation from 1991-92 to 1997-98 and also analyze the revenue composition of union indirect taxes *i.e.* custom duties and excise duties which would provide useful support for evaluation of the process of liberalization. The analysis of revenue from indirect taxes brings out clearly the fact that there is decline role of indirect taxes. In particular, the decline in the share of union excise is the one. Whereas, the revenue from import duties has also gone up. The study also analyzes the commodity wise excise revenue and a commodity wise analysis of revenue from these levies. It points out the fact that the capital goods, inputs and raw materials are subject to heavy burden and the work also elaborate some implication to make liberalization effective and beneficial.

Mittal, J.K. (2001): 'Widening of Service Tax: Union Budget 2001', *Chartered Secretary*; Vol. XXXI (4), A99-A100.

The present paper discusses the changes proposed to be made through the Finance Bill 2001. In the year 2001, 15 new services were added in the list of Service Tax *i.e.* scientific or technical consultancy services, photography services, convention services, leased circuit services, telegraph services, telex services, facsimile (fax) services, on line information and data base access and or retrieval services, video tape production services, sound recording services, broadcasting services, insurance auxiliary services, banking and other financial services, port services and services of repair of automobiles. The present paper deals with each services and some other changes hey are higher interest for delay in payment of tax, penalty levied for non-registration, modification in assessment procedure *etc.*.

Venugopalan, Dr. M.G. (2001): 'Service Tax: A Tax of the Future; *Chartered Secretary*', Vol. XXI(9), 1038-1039.

The present study underlines a number of reasons to justify the taxation of services. First the contribution of service sector which contributed around 50 percent (presently 55 per cent) of the GDP. Second the growth rate of economic activities in the service sector is very fast. Third in developed economies consumption of both goods and services are treated alike and lastly, the revenue receipts from Customs and Excise are on decline. In developed economies consumption of goods and services are treated alike and the revenue receipts from customs and excise are on the decline due to WTO commitments and rationalization of commodity duties. Extending the tax base to the service sector is necessary to improve the revenue productivity and efficiency of our domestic tax system. The paper also deals with the legal base of service taxation, salient features of service tax and future trends of Service Tax in India.

Parsuraman, K.(2001): 'Service Tax: The Tax of the Future', *Chartered Secretary*, Vol. XXI(9), 1043-1046.

The present study explained the salient aspects of the Service Tax. It also explains the administrative mechanism of Service Tax in detail. It also deals with the genesis of Service Tax in India, constitutional and legal provisions behind levy of Service Tax in our country, analyze the views of expert committee on Service Tax. The author also explains the problem before the Service Tax administration in India. It is also envisaged as the tax of future. It emphasizes that the service sector has come to occupy a very important position in the nation's economy and over the year's its potential to contribute to the revenue of the Union are being exploited fully. Service Tax was introduced in our country in a limited way and it now covers a wide spectrum of services.

Rao, M. Govinda (2001): 'Taxing Services: Issues and Strategy', *Economic and Political Weekly*, Vol. 24(36), 3999-4006.

This paper examines the major policy and implementation issues in the taxation of services in India. The paper identifies the important issues in taxation of services with a view to improve the revenue productivity of tax system, ensure a measure of neutrality in taxation between goods and services and eventually help to evolve an efficient system of domestic trade taxes at central and state levels The paper examines the rationale for extending taxation to the services and also discusses designing and implementing the service taxation to enable a coordinated development of domestic trade taxes at central and state levels. It also suggested steps to be taken ahead such as comprehensive approach of taxing services instead of selective taxation. It also discusses prevailing status on taxation of services at central level and development of service sector in 1990s.

Mukhopadhyay, Sukumar (2003): 'Kelkar Committee on Indirect Taxes: A Critique of Final Report', *Economic and Political Weekly*, January 4, 03. 9-14

The present paper describes the different aspects of the final report given by Kelkar Committee on Indirect Taxes. The report has many excellent points but also some defective concepts. The author tried to give emphasize on these aspects. The Kelkar Committee's final report on indirect taxes shows impressive clarity in its tariff proposals. It provides ample evidence of the fact that much thought have been giving in the framing of the recommendations. However, in respect of administrative and procedural aspects the committee has chosen to ignore many of the useful suggestions that had been made in response to its earlier consultation paper. The committee gives some drastic suggestions related to service tax such as comprehensive service tax should be imposed rather than an item wise tax. All new services should be defined properly. Many of the services will not yield much revenue. The collection cost will be heavy compared to revenue yield.

Subramanion, P & Raju, G. (2003): 'Service Tax: A Bird's Eye View', *Southern Economist*, Vol.41(19), 17-18.

The present study deals with the different aspects of service tax such as need for Service Tax, legal base of the tax, salient features, procedures, penalty and interest, appeal and revision *etc.*. It also considered that in the coming years by extending the ambit of Service Tax through including more services in the organized sector. It would enable to collect larger revenue. It highlights that a prominent feature of the growing economic development of India is an upsurge in the emergence of service sector which involve a very heterogeneous spectrum of economic activities. The share of service sector in the real GPD in India has surpassed that of agriculture and industry at a relatively faster pace as compared to other industrialized nations.

Bagchi, Ameresh (2004): 'Taxing Services: The Way Forward', *Economic and Political Weekly*, Vol. 39(19), 1876.

The present paper deals with the issue whether the evolution of the structure of taxation of services is on the right track and also discuses important issues related to its export. The present paper indicates that the services are accounted for the largest share in the GDP and therefore the case for service taxation established. The Union Service Tax in India was introduced in 1994 only on these services and much more services were added in the tax net. The revenue collection also rises in few years. This is because the growth of service sector in the Indian economy has been spectacular in the last 10 years.

Singhal, P.D. (2004): 'Service Tax and Classification of Services', *The Management Accountant*, Vol. 39 (11). 915-917.

The present study on service tax describes the reasons for levying Service Tax, role of service sector in our economy, revenue collection from the tax, charge of Service Tax *etc.*.it also discuss various laws governing Service Tax such as Chapter V of Finance Act, 1994 (Section 64 to 96), Service Tax Rules, 1994, CENVAT Credit Rules, 2004 *etc.*. Besides these the present work also discusses the classification of services as the goods are classified in the Central Excise Tariff Act, 1985 into various headings and sub-headings. In the context of these rules and regulations. The services required to be classified into two or more categories for the convenience of levy of tax. The study also discusses certain important aspects of levying the tax on services.

Acharya, Shankar (2005): 'Thirty Years of Tax Reform in India', *Economic and Political Weekly*, Vol. 40(20), 2061-2070

This paper sketches the contours of India's tax reform story from the mid 1970s to the present and finds that enormous progress has been made in the last 30 years. The present paper has been divided into VI parts. Section I outlines the prevailing consensus regarding the desirable elements of a modern national tax system and compare this model with the Indian reality of the mid 1970s. Section II summarizes the first wave of reforms from 1974 to 1984 which focussed on the direct tax structure. Section III describes the salient features of the important tax reforms launched by V.P.Singh during his two years term as finance minister *i.e.* from 1985-87. Section IV deals with the reforms implemented during the 1990s by successive ministers Manmohan Singh, P.Chidambram and Yashwant Sinha. Many of these reforms were influenced strongly by the seminal Tax Reform Committee Report of 1991-92. Section V summarises the main initiatives undertaken since 2000, some of them have strayed from the vision of Chelliah Committee. Section VI outlines the unfinished agenda for tax reform in India.

Bhatia, Dr. Sitesh (2005): 'Service Tax and Its Justification', *Executive Chartered Secretary*, Vol.11(8), 739-740.

This paper justifies the levying of Service Tax on the basis of efficiency in resource allocation. Resources are liable to be shifted to the sector untaxed. She also justifies it on the ground of equity. She argues that only rich consumes services and if they go without tax the result will be inequlity in income and wealth. The present study also deals with the legislation of service tax, its exemption and constitutional aspects *etc.*. The scope and extent of service tax has been considerably widened year by year and now a very large number of services have been brought under the purview of this tax yielding considerable revenues to the exchequer.

Vinayagamoorthy, A. (2005): 'Service Tax Act: Areas Covered in India', *Southern Economist*, Vol.44(6), 13-14

The present study describe administration of the tax, constitutional validity of tax, legislative history, revenue collection from service tax and basic features of Service Tax such as penalty for non-registration, electronic filling of the return, uniform tax rate, no registration charges *etc.*. Services in India have been showing a tremendous upswing in growth and have by and large, outplayed even the manufacturing sector in terms of growth in the past few years. Service Tax is an indirect tax to be borne by the ultimate consumer client. The service provider cannot claim exemption on the ground that client has paid the tax and would be obliged to collect the same from the customers.

Bagchi Ameresh and Poddar Satya (2006): 'The Long Road Ahead to GST'; *Economic Times*, Wed 18th October, at 8.

The present paper examines the future of Indian tax structure as and after the implementation of GST in 2010. The authors have suggested dual GST model as the most suitable model for India. This will be the combination of state and central GSTs. For this they have also suggested constitutional amendment to empower both the government for the levying of GST. But some of the economist and lawyers are not in favour of the dual GST. They have suggested implementing signal rated GST both at Centre and State level.

Das, Gupta (2007): 'Service Tax—An Overview'. *Service Tax Today*; Vol.9(6), 138-142.

This article gives a panoramic view of service tax since its introduction till the proposal of budget 2007. The author besides tracing the exhibition of Service Tax since its inception highlights its future course and challenges to be faced. The study also clear its international scenario and is of the view that Service Tax is envisaged as the tax of the future, the inclusion of all value added services in the tax net would certainly yield a larger amount of revenue and make existing tax structure more elastic. There are lots of challenges which Service Tax faces such as services unlike goods do not have any physical form (intangible). They are not capable of abstraction and consumption in the sense of goods. They cannot be returned once rendered. Thus, it is a complex task to determine the precise nature of any service which still exists. But beside these complexities Service Tax was introduced in our country in the year 1994 and roots are gaining strength as the time goes on.

Sherry Dr. A.M. (2007): 'Goods and Service Tax (GST) in India—A Move Towards Tax Reforms'; *Service Tax Today*, Vol.7 (5),121-126

This paper deals with the recommendations made by Kelkar Task Force in respect of GST (Goods and Service Tax). The author makes a pointer to the requirement of harmonization of Central and State VAT and while highlighting the significant aspect of VAT. He opines that benefits of VAT will be reaped only when Central Sales Tax (CST) is phased out and Goods and Service Tax is brought into picture. According to the Finance Minister, roadmap for a Goods and Service Tax to replace excise duty and service tax is being prepared and it is hoped that it would be implemented by 2010. With this the indirect tax regime is undergoing a change and in the coming year, the tax reforms will centre on an efficient and harmonized consumption tax system. For increasing the tax revenue and for streaming the tax system, VAT at Central level and State level would gradually move towards Goods and Service Tax.

Pattabhiraman, V. (2007): 'Service to Self is Not Liable to Service Tax', *Service Tax Today*, Vol.6 (5),121-123

In this study the author explains the two different decisions of the court. The conclusion emanating from the two decisions are summarized as—for levy of Service Tax, there should be a service provider and a service receiver, both of them must be distinct and different entities and if one unit of an entity renders any service to another unit of the same entity, it amounts to rendering service to one's own self for which, apart from there being no principal—client relationship, no valuable consideration is received by the principal.

Nathani, Gopal (2007): "Rendition of Service from India *vs.* Services Delivered Outside India', *Service Tax Today*; Vol.7(6),155-158.

In this article the author has drawn a clear distinction between services rendered in India, so that the deduction is limited to consideration received only for services rendered outside India and not in respect of services rendered in India. It emphasized that export of service is exempt from the payment of service tax if service is delivered outside India and payment for such services is received by service provider in convertible foreign exchange. Considering the difficulties in establishing the fact that service is delivered outside India, the Export of Services Rules 2005, have been amended for the second time *w.e.f.* 1.3.2007. Now the service provider is not liable to establish through evidence that the service has been either delivered or received outside India. Rendition of services from India assumes greater significance than delivery or receipt of service outside India in the new regime.

Agarwal, Pawan (2007) : 'Service Tax on Entertainment and Media Industry', *Service Tax Today*, Vol.9(8), 182-187

This study focus on the imposition of service tax on entertainment and media industry. Various aspects related to this industry such as the definition of entertainment, various services that come under the entertainment and media industry such as advertisement, broadcasting, cable operator services, event management, internet café, photography, sound recording, T.V. and radio programme production, video tape production services *etc.* have been discussed in this study. The paper concludes that we are living in an entertainment economy and this is vastly becoming the engine of growth of the economy.

Verma Anubha(2008) : 'Goods and Service Tax : Eagerly Awaited in India", *Service Tax Today*; Vol.15(3), 44-60

This paper examines the advantages of Goods and Service Tax system and the need to implement GST, how this system work, what would be its implications and the various problem likely to be faced by the Central Government while introducing this tax. In the opinion of the author, the dual GST model with a single rate of GST should be adopted rather than different rates for goods and services. The author also describes the impact on consumers, manufacturers and revenue. It also describes experiences of other countries and global practices. In practice most of the countries are having single rate of GST while Indonesia has five positive rates. It emphasized that GST is a multi-stage consumption tax imposed on a broad range of goods and services. 13th Finance Commission is preparing a roadmap for the introduction of the GST.

Rasure, K.A. (2008) : 'Growing Services Sector Under WTO Regime', *Southern Economist*, Vol. 46 (21), 15-17.

The present study deals with the role of service sector in India and also study the growth track of service sector in India. The service sector should make their best efforts in making the required boost to the firm. As there is intense competition in the service sector, the firms should try to come out with innovative measures and schemes for fulfilling and satisfying long term relationship. This is a key success factor for the service sector. It also point out that service sector is highly competitive with the hyper competition setting into the industry. To survive and succeed in this sector, firms have to find out varied ways to be more and more competitive. The sector is becoming more and more customer centric as they have become the major deciding force for the existence itself.

Purohit C. Mahesh and Purohit Vishnu Kant (2010) : 'Goods and Service Tax in India: An Empirial Analysis of Revenue Implication", *The Indian Economic Journal*, Vol. 58, No. 1, 33-59.

Introduction to goods and service tax (GST) surfaces two important issues. First the centre is presently collecting 63 per cent of countries resources. Any major change in the allocation of resources would further erode the autonomy of the States. Second give the base of the tax, what rate would be revenue neutral for both Centre and State? With a view to finding an answer, the present paper adopts different approaches and presents revenue estimates for the period of 2010-11 to 2014-15. Three approaches (*viz.* revenue approach, turnover approach and consumption approach) have been adopted to estimate the revenue. Finally, the study suggest that GST would generate sufficient revenue if we adopt eight per cent standard rate with four per cent reduced rate on a few select necessities.

First Discussion Paper on Goods and Service Tax in India (2009).

The Empowered Committee of State Finance Ministers has submitted their First Discussion Paper on GST on November 10, 2009. The Discussion paper is divided into four sections. Section 1 begins with a brief reference to the process of introduction of VAT at the Centre and the States and also indicates the precise points where there is a need for further improvement. This section also shows how the GST can bring about this improvement. Section 2 then describes the process of preparation for GST. Section 3 presents in detail the comprehensive structure of the GST model. In the end an Annexure on Frequently Asked Questions and answer were also help in illustrating the GST model.

REFERENCES

1. Initially the percentage was set with reference to national income and NDP. However since fifth plan onwards it is used to be calculated as percentage of GDP.

A Brief Review of the Tax Structure in India

INTRODUCTION

The origin of taxation could be traced to the ancient period of human civilization and development. The *Bali,* an oldest form of taxation was found to be the primary source of government revenue during Vedic period. It is referred to be a local tax of one tenth or one twentieth of the agricultural produce. The *Manusmriti* also refers a general levy of one sixth of agriculture production payable for the governance of the community. The source of modern form of Service Tax may be traced to *Kautilya's Arthasastra.* Beside ancient India a satisfactory regime of taxation could also be found in the ancient history of Egypt, Greece and Roman civilizations. The traditional functions of any form of government were defence and maintenance of law and order and for that it required finances. These finances came from the composite groups subject to governance. It was essentially a voluntary contribution for meeting the collective needs of community concerned. A panoramic view of the various studies on public finance one finds that from ancient period till the British period including Mauryan and Mughal period. The main source of public finance was in the shape of income tax, excise duty and land revenue. Tax on transaction is a new phenomenon.

In modern times, the taxing power in India was systematically laid out in the Government of India Act, 1935. There, as a part of scheme of governance the legislative power between federal and provinces were distributed in the Seventh Schedule. List I of the federal legislative list dealt with the power of the Central Government, List II Provincial legislative list and the List III the concurrent list. The same structure was adopted in a modified form in the Seventh Schedule of the Constitution of India.

The Constitution of India Chapter I of part XII deals with finance. In Article 265 embodies an important constitutional principle that 'No tax shall be levied or collected except by the authority of law.' Law here means statutory law *i.e.* the tax cannot be imposed merely by resolution of a house or by any administrative action. The law must be constitutionally valid and should not be violative of any restrictions provided in various Article of the constitution. The law making power including the taxing power is well defined under the Constitution in three Lists of the Seventh Schedule. In the List I dealing with Union Governments power there are fifteen subjects enumerated on which the tax can be levied. The specific entries dealing with taxes are e. 81 to 92 and 92A, 92B and 92C. over and above there is another entry 97 which empowers the Union Government with the residuary power[1] to impose tax not mentioned in List II and List III. In the Seventh Schedule List II dealing with subjects enumerated on whom the states can levy tax. The entries dealing with the taxes are e. 45 to 63. See Table 3.1

Table 3.1 : Distribution of Taxing Power between Centre and State under Constitution of India

List I- Union List			List II- State List		
Sl. No.	Entry No.	Taxing Power	Sl. No.	Entry No.	Taxing Power
1	2	3	4	5	6
1.	82	Taxes on income other than agricultural income	1	45	Land revenue
2.	83	Duties of custom including export duties	2.	46	Taxes on agricultural income
3.	84	Duties of excise except on alcoholic liquors and narcotics but including medicinal and toilet preparation containing alcohol	3.	47	Duties in respect of succession to agricultural land
4.	85	Corporation tax	4.	48	Estate duty in respect of agriculture
5.	86	Taxes on the capital value of assets, exclusive of agricultural land, of individual	5.	49	Taxes on lands and buildings
6.	87	Estate duty in respect of property other than agricultural land	6.	50	Taxes on mineral rights subject to any limitations imposed by Parliament by law relating to mineral development
7.	88	Duties in respect of succession to property other	7.	51	Duties on excise on alcoholic liquors and narcotics

(Contd...)

1	2	3	4	5	6
		than agricultural land			manufactured or produced in the State but not including medicinal and toilet preparations containing alcohol
8.	89	Terminal taxes on goods and passengers carried by railway, sea or air; taxes on railway fares and freights	8.	52	Taxes on the entry of goods into a local area for consumption, use or sale therein
9.	90	Taxes other than stamp duties on transaction in stock exchanges and future markets	9.	53	Taxes on consumption or sale of electricity
10.	91	Rates of stamp duty in respect of bills of exchange, cheques, promissory notes, bills of lading, letter of credit, policies of insurance, transfer of shares, debentures, proxies and receipts	10.	54	Taxes on the sale or purchase of goods other than newspapers, subject to the provisions of entry 92A of List I
11.	92	Taxes on the sale or purchase of newspapers and on advertisement published therein	11.	552	Taxes on advertisements other than advertisements published in the newspapers (and advertisement broadcast by radio or television)

(Contd...)

1	2	3	4	5	6
12.	92A[3]	Taxes on the sale or purchase of goods other than newspapers, where such sale or purchase takes place in the course of inter-State trade or commerce	12.	56	Taxes on goods and passengers carried by road or inland waterways
13.	92B[4]	Taxes on the consignment of goods (whether the consignment is to the person making it or to any other person), where such consignment take place in the course of inter-State trade or commerce	13.	57	Taxes on vehicles, whether mechanically propelled or not, suitable for use on roads, including tram cars subject to the provisions of Entry 35 of List III.
14.	92C[5]	Taxes on services	14.	58	Taxes on animals and boats
15.	97	Any tax not enumerated in List II or List III of the Seventh Schedule	15.	59	Tolls
			16.	60[6]	Taxes on professions, trades, calling and employment.
			17	61	Capitation taxes
			18.	62	Taxes on luxuries, including taxes on entertainment, amusements, betting and gambling

(Contd...)

1	2	3	4	5	6
			19	63	Rates of stamp duty in respect of documents other than those specified in the provisions of List I with regard to rates of stamp duty

Source: Government of India, Ministry of Law, Justice and Company Affairs, the Constitution of India, Seventh Schedule, List I and II.

It was apply pointed out in the report of Tax Reform Committee 1991:

> The power to levy a tax on services in general is not mentioned either in the Union List or in the State List in the VII schedule of the Constitution. However by virtue of Entry 1997 in the Union List which gives power to the Centre for levy and collection of "any tax not mentioned in either of those Lists" (that is, the State List or the Concurrent List), it is clear that the Union Legislature is competent to levy indirect tax on services[7].

CLASSIFICATION OF TAXES: DIRECT AND INDIRECT

Taxes are traditionally classified by classical economist. The classification of taxes into direct and indirect made by classical economics writer (Dalton, Mill, Macro, Basteble) it continues to be followed by modern economist A.R. Prest and so on... The classification was made on the bases of their incidence and the technique of shifting into direct and indirect taxes. Direct taxes are income tax, corporation tax, wealth tax etc.. Indirect tax, on the other hand are custom duty, excise duty, service tax etc.. To a greater extend this classification serves the purpose of understanding the nature and function of various taxes. However, this distinction is merely a theoretical and of academic value only. There are certain taxes which can not be put strictly under this classification. Modern economist like Musgrave and Hicks do not adopt the classical approach.

The constitution of India do not use the term direct or indirect. It refers them as taxes on income, taxes on capital, land revenue, taxes on capital and so on in the Seventh Schedule List I and List II where the taxing power is provided. Constitution is concerned only with the validity and constitutionality of a tax measure. The Supreme Court of India confronted with this issue of classification. It specifically rejected to accept the classical classification of taxes into direct and indirect.

Direct taxes are those, which are paid by the taxpayers directly from their income. The Government collects direct taxes, directly from the taxpayers through levies such as income tax, corporation tax, wealth tax and interest tax. Gift tax and Estate duty were also part of the direct tax revenue. However, in an ongoing process of simplification and rationalization of direct tax structure in India, the Government repealed the Estate Duty Act in the late eighties and Gift Tax Act in 1998. Direct taxes are considered practically harsh and form a minor part of Government's revenue.

Indirect taxes are those taxes, which are paid by the taxpayers indirectly when purchasing some goods or commodity and when hiring some services, which are taxable; these taxes are although borne by taxpayers, but not paid by them directly to the Government. Excise Duty, Custom Duty, Service Tax, Sales Tax, Octroi, Entry Tax, Luxury Tax, Trade Tax, Consignment Tax, Value Added Tax (VAT), Property Tax *etc.* are the examples of indirect taxes.

In today's global market, indirect taxes have assumes great significance and can affect every link in the supply chain, both domestically and internationally, since one person's sale is another's purchase and one country's export is another's import. Indirect taxes are levied on manufacture of goods, import of goods into India, entry of goods into local territory, purchase of goods, hiring of services *etc.*. Indirect tax is paid before the goods reach in the hands of taxpayers or services are enjoyed by him. These taxes are levied at the time of manufacture of goods or their transfer from one hand to another.

The cost of collection of indirect taxes is much less than the cost of collection of direct taxes. The tax evasion is also much less in case of indirect taxes, due to simplicity of procedures and convenience of control. It is comparatively easier to detect tax evasion in case of indirect taxes, as compare to evasion in case of direct taxes. Indirect taxes play significant role in planning, industrial growth and encouraging setting of industries in selected backwards areas by offering concession, rebates and holidays.

The role of indirect taxes is also important in regulating international trade completion by levying Custom Duties in accordance with the domestic needs. By levy of high Custom Duty and Anti-dumping Duty the Government control import of goods into India and thus, provides protection to the trade and industry in India. They also help in regulating wasteful expenditure by levying taxes on items of luxury, like Luxury Tax *etc.*. This helps the Government even in setting directions for industrial growth, by regulating demand as well as import and export. Payment of indirect taxes is made by a taxpayer at the time purchase of goods or as if he is paying something as additional cost. Thus, taxpayer's psychology favours indirect taxes. The assessee of indirect taxes i.e. much attention on indirect tax planning as they do in case of direct tax planning. Thus manufactures psychology also favours indirect taxes.

Indirect tax is levied on goods and services. This increases the price of goods, commodities and services. Therefore indirect taxes are called inflationary. The incidence of indirect taxes is uniform without discrimination. It does not distinguish between rich and poor. Direct taxes are progressive while indirect taxes are regressive and the burden of these taxes lies ultimately on the poor. While the indirect taxes provide the Government, a measure to regulate international competition with domestic industries and provide protection,, they render the domestic industries lethargic and lacking quality consciousness, which ultimately costs high on consumers.

In developing economy the characteristic feature is that the more revenue is derives from indirect taxes because the number of assessee is less and per capita income is low. Therefore, more stress is given on indirect taxes. On the other hand in developed economies as the per capita income is high and number of taxpayers is large. Therefore more revenue can be raised through direct levies. As economy moves from developing towards developed the proportion of direct taxes is gradually increasing in comparison of indirect taxes.

TAXES LEVIED BY THE CENTRAL GOVERNMENT

Income Tax: When the tax is levy on income of a person, it is called income tax. The term 'income' is of widest amplitude. Any amount received by a person from whatever sources will qualify as income and liable to tax unless otherwise specified in the Income-Tax Laws. 'Income for income tax proposes includes salary, profits and gain, dividend, voluntary contribution, value of any perquisite of profit in lieu of salary, special allowance or benefit, capital gains, winnings from lotteries, horse races, card games *etc.*. The incidence of burden of income tax is on the person who pays the tax.

The income tax levied is under the Income Tax Act of 1961 as amended from time to time. This Act provides that income tax would be charged for any assessment year at the relevant rate on the total income would include all income derived from different sources, which:

(*a*) Is received or is deemed to be received in India in such year by or on behalf of such person; or (*b*) Accrues or arises or is deemed to accrue or arise to him in India during such year; or

(*c*) Accrue or arises to him outside India during such year.

It is provided that, in the case of a person not ordinarily resident in India the income which accrues or arises to him outside India shall not be so included unless it is derived from a business controlled in or a profession set up in India. The present Income tax rate structure, as specified by the 2008-09 Budget is as follows:

Income in Rs.	Income Tax rate
Up to Rs. 1,50,000	Nil
Rs. 150,001 to Rs. 300,000	10 per cent
Rs. 300,001 to Rs. 500,000	20 per cent
Rs. 500,001	30 per cent

The Income Tax Act is proposed to be redrafted in the year 2010.

Corporation Tax: Tax levied on the taxable income of a company is called corporation tax. A corporation is legal identity separate from its owners i.e. the stock holders. The corporation pays a tax on its net income while stock-holder pay a tax on dividend income under the individual income tax. In other word, dividends are not a deductable expense for the corporation. Before 1959-60, the super tax on companies was known as the corporation tax. In 1960-61, income tax on companies was also included in the corporation tax. Further in 1965, these two taxes were integrated into one 'Corporation Tax'. In short, corporation tax is paid out of the taxable profits (net profit) after meeting all costs i.e. interest charges, wages and depreciation cost etc. earned by the corporation during an assessment year and the remaining is to be distributed among the shareholders.

Central Excise Duty: Central Excise Duty is levied and collected on all excisable goods other than salt which are produced or manufactured in India. The taxing event is manufacture or production though duty is collected at the time of clearance. The list of excisable goods has been specified in the Schedule to the Central Excise Tariff. The various types of statues for levy of duties of excise or representing such duties are as below:

- Duty of Excise specified in First Schedule or Second Schedule to the Central Excise Tariff Act, 1985.
- Additional Duty of Excise leviable under section 3 of the additional duties of excise (Textiles and textiles articles) Act, 1978.
- Additional duty of excise under the additional duties of excise (goods of special importance) Act, 1957.
- National calamity contingent duty leviable under section 136 of the Finance Act, 2001.
- Educational cess on excisable goods/ services leviable under section 91 read with 93 and 95 of the Finance (No.2) Act, 2004.
- The secondary and higher educational cess on excisable goods and services leviable under section 136 read with section 138 and 140 of the Finance Act, 2007.
- Additional duty leviable under section 3 of Customs Tariff Act, equivalent to the duty of excise specified in 1 to 5 of Finance Act, 2007.
- Additional duty of excise leviable under sub- section (5) of section 3 of Customs tariff Act, but this not available to input used by a service provider.
- Additional duty of excise leviable under section 157 of the Finance Act, 2003.
- The additional duty of excise leviable under section 85 of the Finance Act 2005 and the Service Tax leviable under section 66 of the Finance Act.

Customs Duty: Duties of customs are levied and collected at such rates as may be specified in the customs tariff on goods imported into or exported from India. If goods are brought into or exported out from a place other than Customs Ports, Air Ports or Inland Customs Station such goods are liable for penal action. The customs frontier is not so well guarded. Therefore attempt to load or unload sensitive cargo in unauthorized places is very much there.

The goods on import are ordinarily assessed under transaction value. The value in such cases is deemed to the price at which such goods are ordinarily sold or offered for sale for deliver at the time and place of importation or exportation in the course of international trade to the country of importation or exportation.

Wealth Tax: Wealth Tax is payable on money value of wealth owned by a person. The tax is payable on net wealth of every individual, Hindu undivided family and company. In computing the net wealth of an individual, the value of assets held by the spouse, minor child or any other person without adequate consideration is included to the value of net wealth of the individual. Wealth tax is not payable by an assessee on any property held by him under trust for any public purpose for a charitable or religious nature in India, interest in coparcenaries property, residential building and jewellary in possession of an assessee who is ex-ruler, assets and debts located outside India *etc.*

At present, value of net wealth on first Rs. 2.5 lakhs is exempt from wealth tax, whereas for a Hindu undivided family such exemption limit is only is Rs.1.5 lakhs.

Gift Tax: When a tax is levied in respect of the gifts, it is called gift-tax. Gift means the transfer by one person to another of any existing movable or immovable property made voluntarily and without consideration is deemed to be gift. Certain gifts are exempted. Movable or immovable properties located outside India are not liable to gift-tax. Similarly gifts under a will in contemplation of death are not taxable.

Payment made up to rupees one lakh only, made at the time of marriage is not liable to tax. Again payment made by an employer to his employees by way of bones, gratuity *etc.* are excluded from the purview of gift tax. At present Gift-Tax is leviable at a flat rate of 30 per cent taxable gift.

Expenditure Tax: the expenditure tax is levied on chargeable expenditure incurred in a hotel or restaurant. The present rate of expenditure tax for room charges in hotel is 10 per cent whereas for expenditure incurred in or payment made to the hotel in connection with the provision of accommodation, food and drink, rent paid towards hire or lease and services like beauty parlour, health club, swimming pool *etc.*. If any payment is received in foreign exchange the same is exempt from tax. When any payment is made by any diplomatic personnel, the same is excluded from chargeable expenditure. Again, the expenditure incurred by foreign tourists through tour operators or foreign agents who may pay the hotel in Indian currency but receive payment for incurring such expenditure in foreign currencies, is not liable to tax.

Similarly, taxable expenditure for a restaurant is the expenditure incurred in or payments made to a restaurant in connection with the provision of food or drink by the restaurant. The person who carries on the business of the hotel or restaurant is liable to pay the tax.

Interest Tax: The interest earned by the credit institution is subjected to interest tax. In this context, interest means interest on loans and advances made in India including commitment charge on utilized portion of any credit sanctioned and discount on promissory notes and bills of exchange. The credit institutions are any bank or banking institution, public financial institution, state financial corporation and any other financial company *i.e.* company engaged in activities like hire purchase, investment, housing finance, loans or advances *etc.*

The chargeable interest for the purpose of Interest Tax is the interest previous year but excluding the interest on loans and advances made to another credit institution and bad debt. The principal officer of the credit institution is responsible for payment of interest tax.

Central Sales Tax: sales tax is levied and collected from registered dealer on sale price of the goods. The case of Central Sales Tax is no different, except that it is levied on Inter- State sales. The registered dealer pays tax under the Act on all sales of goods other than electrical energy affected by him in course of inter-state trade or commerce.

A sale or purchase of goods shall be deemed to take place in the course of inter-state trade or commerce if such sale or purchase occasions the movement of goods from State to another or is affected by a transfer of documents of title to the goods during the movement from one State to another. Liability to Central Sales tax is not dependent liability to Sales Tax in the appropriate State.

Central Sales Tax is levied by the Central Government but the tax so levied is collected by the appropriate State, *i.e.* the State in which the registered dealer is located. When the registered dealer is located in more than one state, then each places of business is treated as separate entity for purpose of levy and collection of the Central Sales Tax.

Service Tax: The Tax Reform Committee 1991 made specific suggestion about taxation of the service sector. By following the recommendation of the Committee tax on specific services were imposed in the Budget 1994-95. The Service Tax has been levied by the Central Government initially it was levied under the residuary power of the Union Government after that in the year 2003 the entry 92C—Taxing on services were added. Service Tax is levied on taxable services provided to any person by the person rendering such service or responsible for collecting the Service Tax. Since the person responsible for collecting the Service Tax is also consuming taxable goods, he gets rebate on taxes paid on such commodities. In our country tax on goods is distinct and different from tax on services.

Goods and Services Tax (GST): GST is a multistage consumption tax imposed on a broad range of goods and services. It is proposed to be implemented from 1st April, 2010. It is a tax on transactions and customers who consume the goods or services bear the final cost of the tax. It is the combination of three taxes namely:

(*a*) Act of manufacture that is excise;

(*b*) Act of a sale that is sales tax or VAT;

(*c*) Act of providing services that is Service Tax.

GST is essentially a value added tax that requires producers to pay tax only on the value add to the goods or services in place of the current system in which Central and State imposts cascade on the price of the final product. It is a tax on goods and services, which is leviable at each point of sales or provision of services.

TAX REFORM IN INDIA

Reform is a continuous process whether it is social, economic or fiscal. Comprehensive tax reform had to be an essential element of any programme of stabilization of economy and structural reform because macroeconomic stabilization requires reduction in fiscal deficit which had to depend more on high tax collection. Therefore direct and indirect tax reforms are necessary.

Indian tax system suffers from various drawbacks such as taxation system is inconsistent and unscientific. As it is not based upon any organized planning and it fails to effect production, investment and savings of the economy in an efficient way. Inelasticity and inflexibility is another drawback of Indian tax system. It leaves agricultural tax out of purview and entirely depends on urban income, thus limiting scope for direct taxation. Moreover indirect tax is also most inelastic in the country which adds more suffering to the poor sections of the society. Thus, it fails to strike a balance between direct and indirect taxes. Tax structure is traditional and conservative then much attention is given to indirect taxes. In other developed country direct taxes are considered most important and having productive effects on the economy. The income derived from taxes is not sufficient to fulfill the needs of the government. The most serious defect of Indian tax system is the defect of tax division. This evil leads to generate black money which create acute problem in the form of parallel economy. Moreover black money is utilized secretly in illegal transaction for earning more and more money. It is evident that Indian tax structure faces many shortcomings which need drastic changes in the whole system. Therefore government took several steps for the improvement of the system and Government of India has appointed various committees, to suggest ways for improving the tax structure in the country. The recommendations of some of the committees are as follows:

RECOMMENDATION OF THE TAX REFORM COMMITTEE (1991)

The tax reform committee was constituted under the chairmanship of Dr. Raja J. Chelliah in 1991 to examine the existing tax structure in the country and make appropriate recommendations to reform it. In its report the committee had recommended far reaching changes in the tax system to remove loop holes besides making it more efficient from revenue raising point of view. There is a consensus among fiscal experts based on experience gained all over the world that a moderately progressive tax structure combined with strong enforcement is the best way encouraging honesty and voluntary tax compliance.

The committee was in favour of making tax system and law relating to taxes quite simple. In tax system there would be limited number of rates and few exemptions or deductions.

Further it would give little discretionary power to the tax officials for interpreting the law. The committee was also of the view that the present method of tax administration needs to be modernized and tax enforcement visibly improved. In respect of particular taxes the Chelliah committee had the following recommendation:

1. In order to make the country's direct tax system more effective it is necessary that the income tax regime has lower rate of taxation with a narrower spread between the entry rate and maximum rate and a minimum rate of tax incentive.
2. The system of subjecting the income of both partnership firm as well as the partners to taxation amounted to double taxation and this should be avoided.
3. Corporation tax rate for domestic companies being high should be lowered to 40 per cent and the surcharge should be abolished. Tax rate for foreign companies should be lowered and the differential between the tax rate on domestic and foreign companies should be around 7.5 per cent points and in no case to exceed 10 per cent points.
4. The prevailing tax treatment of long term capital gains was not correct because the deduction allowed in computing taxable gains were not related to the period of time for which the assets were held. It also did not take into account the inflation that might have occurred over time. A system of indexation had to be adopted to take care of the problem.
5. For levying wealth tax distinction is to be made between productive and non-productive assets, by exempting productive assets such as shares, securities, bonds, bank deposits, etc. from the wealth tax the government can encourage the investment in them.

6. The Chelliah committee, which was asked to look into all aspects of custom duties, recommended reduction in general level of tariffs, reduction in the dispersion of the tariff rate and a rationalization of the system with abolition of numerous end-use exemptions and concessions. It also suggested that the process of reform should be gradual, so as to moderate the revenue loss and the pace at which the industry is exposed to competition.
7. At present excise duty is levied on ad valorem basis on some of the commodities and at specific rates on others. Over the years for administrative reasons, *ad valorem* duties have been steadily replaced by specific duties. Ad valorem duties are preferable to specific duties as they ensure buoyancy in revenue on account of increase in prices. Underlining this fact the committee recommended switching over to *ad valorem* rates for a number of commodities. It also suggested that where specific rates have to be retained. The same should be revised every year taking into account the price inflation.
8. The committee also suggested implementing the tax on specified five services.

IMPLEMENTATION OF CHELLIAH COMMITTEE RECOMMENDATION

The basic philosophy underlying this recommendation is to cut through the welter of detailed changes which were made over the year to serve narrow objective and restore the tax system to its primary function of generating revenues in an efficient manner. The government agreeing with this approach decided to implement the recommendations of the Chelliah Committee in phased manner. The major changes which have already been made in the direct and indirect tax policies are stated below:

Direct Taxes: Personal income tax has been restructured with lower taxes, fewer slabs, and a higher exemption limit and reduced saving linked tax exemptions. The system of taxation of firms has been rationalized and unregistered firms and flat rate of tax of 35 per cent has been prescribed on all partnerships. Reforms in the area of corporate taxes were postponed for the time being because of the limited room for maneuverability in the area of direct taxes.

However, the Corporation Tax rate was brought down to 35 per cent for domestic company and to 40 per cent for foreign company. Taxation of capital gains has been restructured so that only capital gains of price increase would be taxed. Long term capital gains will now be taxed at flat rates after making adjustment for inflation in the cost of asset. The wealth tax has also been reformed by changing the basis of taxation from wealth to unproductive assets.

Indirect Taxes: In realm of indirect taxation the Government considered Customs Duty to be the critical area and thus duties were reduced. For the year 2003, the peak level of Custom Duty has been scaled down to 25 per cent. However, the revised rates of Customs Duty are still higher than in most of our competitor countries especially on capital goods. The reforms in Excise Duties have been guided by the need to simplify the rate structure, to give some relief on articles of mass consumption, help the domestic capital goods industries so as to increase its competitiveness and also reduced capital costs, assist industries suffering from depress demand condition and to provide relief to small scale industries. The Excise Duty structure was rationalized to a single rate 16 per cent CENVAT in 2000-01. Considering rationalization of excise rate structure and reduction of the multiplicity of rates as integral to the total tax reform process, the Budget for 2003-04 has prescribe three-tier excise duty structure of 8 per cent, 16 per cent and 24 per cent.

Service Tax: In the Budget for 1994-95 a tax on three specified services *viz.* telephone, general insurance and stock broker was introduced, at present more than hundred specified service attracted service tax levy. The reason for levying the Service Tax as follows:

- As the share of services in GDP expands while that of industry declines, the tax base shrinks and the excise GDP ratio falls. This requires taxation of services.
- Failure to tax services causes distortion in consumer's choice as it encourages spending or services at the expenses of goods.
- Most of the services that become taxable are the once that are availed by the high income house holds. Hence, subjecting them to taxation may improve equity.
- If services are not taxed, traders cannot claim VAT on their service inputs. This is likely to cause cascading, distort choice and encourage business in-house services.

TASK FORCE ON DIRECT AND INDIRECT TAXES (2002)

Two Task force were set up in September 2002 under the Chairmanship of Vijay L.Kelkar, advisor to minister of finance and company affairs to recommend measures for simplification and rationalization of direct and indirect taxes. The Task Forces submitted their final reports to the government in December 2002. These Task Forces have made important recommendation on improving tax administration which should be both simple and effective and at par with international standards.

Major recommendations of the Task Force on Direct Taxes are as follows:

1. For toning up administration the Task Force on direct taxes recommended:
   - Expansion of tax payer services both qualitatively;
   - Extension of PAN to cover all economic agents/ citizens;
   - Processing of all returns and issue of refunds with four months;
   - Introduction of transparency and objectivity in the process of selection of cases; and
   - Enhancing accountability of officers and staff.
2. In respect of personal income tax the Task Force recommended:
   - Increase in exemption limit to Rs.1 lakh for the general categories of tax payers and higher exemption limit Rs. 1.5 lakh for widow and senior citizens;
   - Introduction of a two rate tax-schedule 20 percent upto an income of Rs. 4 lakh and 30percent for income exceeding Rs. 4 lakh; and
   - Elimination of standard deduction and tax incentives under section 88, 80 and interest income section under section 10.
3. In respect of corporation tax the Task Force recommended:
   - Reduction in tax rate to 30 per cent for domestic companies and to 35 per cent for foreign companies;
   - Reduction in general rate of depreciation for plant and machinery to 15 per cent from the existing 25 per cent;

- Elimination of minimum alternate tax; and
- Long term capital gains to be aggregated with other incomes and subjected to taxation at the normal rates.

4. Abolition of wealth tax.

The Task Force on indirect taxes made the following major recommendation:

1. In order to tone up tax administration the Task Force on indirect taxes recommended:
    - Customs clearance to be based on trust and to be uniformly applied to all importer and exporter;
    - Time limit for processing an import or export document;
    - Levy of Central Excise to be progressively based upon processing stage;
    - CENVAT credit rules to be attended to abolish district ion between capital goods and inputs;
    - All Customs and Central Excise Commissionerate to fully automate their process by January, 2004.
2. In respect of customs duty the Task Force on indirect taxes recommended:
    - Multiplicity of levies to be reduced to three, *viz.* basic customs duty, additional duty of customs and anti-dumping duties;
    - Substantial duty reduction-zero per cent duty on items like life saving drugs and equipments, sovereign imports and imports by RBI, 10 per cent duty on raw materials, input and intermediate goods and 20 per cent duty on consumer goods by 2004-05, five per cent duty on basic raw materials like cost, eight per cent duty for intermediate goods, 10 per cent duty on finished goods other than consumer durable and

20 percent on consumer durables by 2006-07. Duty reduction to the level of 5-10 per cent should start after the introduction of State level VAT;

- A duty eight per cent on crude oil and 15 per cent on petroleum products from 2004-05;
- Higher duty up to 150 per cent on specified agricultural products; and
- All exemptions to be removed except in the case of life saving goods, goods of security and strategic interest, goods for relief and charitable purpose and international obligations.

3. In case of Central Excise Duty the Task Force on indirect taxes recommended:
   - All levies to be reviewed and to and to be replaced by only one levy *i.e.* the CENVAT;
   - Zero excise duty on life items and agricultural products, six per cent for processed food products and matches, 14 per cent standard rate for a items not mentioned against other rates, 20 per cent on motor vehicles, air conditions and aerated water;
   - A uniform rate of 16 per cent on all fibers and yarns;
   - All exemptions to be removed on the textile sector except for fabrics woven handloom and certified as khadi;
   - Duty exemption in respect of small units with turnover of Rs. 50 lakh;
   - Uniformity in all State legislation and procedures relating to VAT.
4. In case of Service Tax the Task Force on indirect taxes recommended:

- Extension of Service Tax in a comprehensive manner leaving out only a few services including them in a negative list;
- There should be complete integration of the Cenvat credit and Service Tax credit schemes with effect from 1.4.2003;
- Credit of Central duties (on goods and services) should be utilized for payment of Service Tax collected and appropriated by Central Government;
- Service Tax should be levied on services, which are received within the country;
- There should be separate legislation to administer the tax;
- It is recommended that the services should be classified on the basis of WTO classification;
- Service Tax should be the first E-tax of the country.

The main recommendation on direct taxes thus rebate to raising of exemption limit of personal income tax, rationalization of exemptions, abolition of concessional treatment to long term capital gain reducing rates of corporate tax and abolition of wealth tax. In respect of indirect taxes, the main recommendations relate to widening of the tax rates and expansion in the coverage of Service Tax. Some of the recommendations of the Task Force were also implemented in the country.

REVENUE COLLECTION FROM DIRECT AND INDIRECT TAXES

In this section we have discussed the revenue collection from direct and indirect taxes and also the receipts of various taxes levied by Union Government.

Table 3.2: Tax Revenue of the Central Government

Revenue (Rs. Crores)

Financial Year	Direct	Indirect
1950-51	176	229
1951-52	190	322
1952-53	186	259
1953-54	166	254
1954-55	161	294
1955-56	171	314
1956-57	194	373
1957-58	230	462
1958-59	238	463
1959-60	269	525
1960-61	292	603
1961-62	337	717
1962-63	423	862
1963-64	550	1084
1964-65	600	1221
1965-66	598	1463
1966-67	657	1650
1967-68	655	1698
1968-69	698	1812
1969-70	826	1996
1970-71	869	2337
1971-72	1047	2826
1972-73	1233	3272
1973-74	1375	3695

(Contd...)

Financial Year	Direct	Indirect
1974-75	1650	4672
1975-76	2205	5404
1976-77	2320	5943
1977-78	2405	6453
1978-79	2528	7997
1979-80	2818	9156
1980-81	2997	10182
1981-82	3786	12061
1982-83	4139	13557
1983-84	4498	16223
1984-85	4798	18673
1985-86	5620	23051
1986-87	6236	26601
1987-88	6752	30914
1988-89	8830	35644
1989-90	10003	41633
1990-91	11030	46547
1991-92	15353	52008
1992-93	18140	56496
1993-94	20299	55443
1994-95	26966	65328
1995-96	33563	77661
1996-97	38891	89871
1997-98	48274	90946
1998-99	46600	97197
1999-2000	57959	113794

(Contd...)

Financial Year	Direct	Indirect
2000-01	68306	120297
2001-02	69196	117863
2002-03	83085	133181
2003-04	105082	149266
2004-05	132761	172197
2005-06	170077	200064
2006-07	210684	231469
2007-08	295938	279031
2008-09(R.E.)	345000	281359

***Source*:** Compiled from Public Finance, CMIE Publication, November 2006, Economic Survey 2008-09

The table is description of the year to year revenue collection from direct and indirect taxes from 1950-51 to 2008-09. In 1950-51the revenue collections from direct taxes were Rs. 176 crores and indirect taxes was Rs. 229 crores. With the span of time the revenue collection from both the taxes increased but the rate of growth of indirect taxes were much more than direct taxes. The average growth rate for first decades (1950-51 to 1960-61) for direct and indirect tax were 6.5 per cent and 16.33 per cent respectively. In the very next decades (1960-61 to 1970-71) the average growth rate for direct taxes was 22.30 per cent and indirect taxes were 287.56 per cent and accounted Rs. 869 crores and Rs. 2337 crores respectively. In the decade of 70s again the average growth rate of indirect taxes was more than the direct taxes. Though, the revenue collections from both the taxes were increasing decade by decade but the collection of revenue from indirect taxes always remained higher ver. direct taxes. After the New Economic Policy of 1991 the direct taxes contribution were started increasing and in the year 2007-08 the revenue collection from direct taxes exceeds over the collection of indirect taxes.

Table 3.3: Tax Revenue of the Central Government

(Percentage Share in Total)

Financial Year	Direct	Indirect
1950-51	43.46	56.54
1951-52	37.11	62.89
1952-53	41.08	58.02
1953-54	39.52	60.48
1954-55	35.38	64.62
1955-56	35.26	64.74
1956-57	34.04	65.96
1957-58	33.95	66.05
1958-59	34.00	66.00
1959-60	33.88	66.12
1960-61	32.63	67.37
1961-62	31.97	68.03
1962-63	32.92	67.08
1963-64	33.66	66.34
1964-65	32.95	67.05
1965-66	29.02	70.98
1966-67	28.48	71.52
1967-68	27.84	72.16
1968-69	27.81	72.19
1969-70	29.27	70.73
1970-71	27.11	72.89
1971-72	27.03	72.97
1972-73	27.37	72.63
1973-74	27.12	72.88
1974-75	26.01	73.09

(Contd...)

Financial Year	Direct	Indirect
1975-76	28.98	71.02
1976-77	28.08	71.92
1977-78	27.15	72.85
1978-79	24.02	75.98
1979-80	23.53	76.47
1980-81	22.74	77.26
1981-82	23.89	76.11
1982-83	23.39	76.61
1983-84	21.71	78.29
1984-85	20.44	79.56
1985-86	19.06	80.04
1986-87	18.99	81.01
1987-88	17.93	82.07
1988-89	19.85	80.15
1989-90	19.37	80.63
1990-91	19.16	80.84
1991-92	22.79	77.21
1992-93	24.03	75.07
1993-94	26.08	73.02
1994-95	28.04	71.06
1995-96	30.02	69.01
1996-97	30.02	69.01
1997-98	34.07	64.05
1998-99	32.04	66.07
1999-2000	33.07	65.05
2000-01	36.02	62.09

(Contd...)

Financial Year	Direct	Indirect
2001-02	37.0	62.1
2002-03	38.4	60.7
2003-04	41.3	57.9
2004-05	43.9	56.1
2005-06	45.9	54.1
2006-07	47.6	52.4
2007-08	49.9	47.0
2008-09	54.9	44. 8

Source: Compiled from Public Finance, CMIE Publication, November 2006, Economic Survey 2008-09

The table indicates the percentage of both the taxes in total tax. The ratio between direct and indirect taxes which stood at 43.46 : 56.54 in 1950-51, with the every passing decade It was recorded 32.63 : 67.37 in 1960-61, 27.11 : 72.89 in 1970-71, 22.74 : 77.26 in 1980-81, 19.16 :80.84 in 1990-91 and 36.2 : 62.9 in 2000-01. This clearly depicts that the percentage share of direct taxes was declining very fast. But after the tax reforms initiated in 1991 the decline in the relative share of direct taxes has not only been arrested but reversed. The ratio between direct and indirect taxes which stood at 19.16 : 80.84 in 1990-91 was changed to 36.2 : 62.9 in 2000-01 and in the year 2007-08 the contribution of direct taxes or the share of direct taxes exceeds indirect taxes. This indicates that the economy is moving towards developed economy from a developing economy.

Table 3.4 : Tax Revenue Of Central Government

(Percentage Share of GDP)

Financial Year	Direct	Indirect
1950-51	1.88	2.45
1951-52	1.91	3.23

(Contd...)

Financial Year	Direct	Indirect
1952-53	1.09	2.65
1953-54	1.56	2.39
1954-55	1.06	2.92
1955-56	1.67	3.06
1956-57	1.59	3.08
1957-58	1.83	3.67
1958-59	1.07	3.03
1959-60	1.82	3.55
1960-61	1.08	3.72
1961-62	1.96	4.17
1962-63	22.29	4.67
1963-64	2.59	5.01
1964-65	2.42	4.93
1965-66	2.29	5.06
1966-67	2.22	5.58
1967-68	1.89	4.91
1968-69	1.09	4.94
1969-70	2.05	4.94
1970-71	2.01	5.41
1971-72	2.26	6.11
1972-73	2.42	6.42
1973-74	2.22	5.96
1974-75	2.25	6.38
1975-76	2.08	6.86
1976-77	2.73	7.00

(Contd...)

Financial Year	Direct	Indirect
1977-78	2.05	6.72
1978-79	2.43	7.68
1979-80	2.46	8.01
1980-81	2.02	7.49
1981-82	2.37	7.55
1982-83	2.32	7.61
1983-84	2.17	7.81
1984-85	2.07	8.07
1985-86	2.14	8.79
1986-87	2.13	9.08
1987-88	2.03	9.28
1988-89	2.23	9.01
1989-90	2.19	9.11
1990-91	2.06	8.69
1991-92	2.49	8.44
1992-93	2.57	8.01
1993-94	2.53	6.92
1994-95	2.06	6.04
1995-96	2.08	6.05
1996-97	2.09	6.05
1997-98	3.02	5.09
1998-99	2.07	5.05
1999-2000	3.00	5.08
2000-01	3.03	5.07
2001-02	3.00	5.01
2002-03	3.04	5.03

(Contd...)

Financial Year	Direct	Indirect
2003-04	3.8	5.3
2004-05	4.3	5.5
2005-06	4.8	5.7
2006-07	5.3	5.9
2007-08	6.3	5.9
2008-09	6.5	5.3

Source: Compiled from Public Finance, CMIE Publication, November 2006, Economic Survey 2008-09

The Table-3.4 indicates the percentage share of direct and indirect taxes in relation to GDP. The share of indirect is always more than the direct taxes. In 1950-51 the share of direct taxes was 1.88 per cent and the share of indirect taxes was 2.45percent. The percentage share of both were increased to 1.80 per cent and 3.72 per cent in 1960-61, 2.01 per cent and 5.41 per cent in 1970-71, 2.20 per cent and 7.49 per cent in 1980-81, 2.06 per cent and 8.69 per cent in 1990-91, 3.01 per cent and 5,1 per cent in 200-01. Indicates that percentage share of direct taxes in GDP were increasing by the rate of growth was very slow from 1.88 per cent in 1950-51 it's increased to 3.3 per cent in 2000-01 within fifty years. After that the growth rate was appreciating and within 6 year's it's touched the figure of indirect taxes. The percentage share of indirect taxes were increased from 2.45 per cent in 1950-51 to 9.11 per cent in 1989-90 but after the introduction of New Economic Policy the share of indirect taxes were start decline and reach to 5.3 per cent in the year 2008-09. All these figures clearly indicate that our economy is moving towards developed economy.

The share of direct and indirect taxes can be evident from the Figure 4.1 also.

TAX REVENUE OF CENTRAL GOVERNMENT: DIRECT AND INDIRECT TAXES

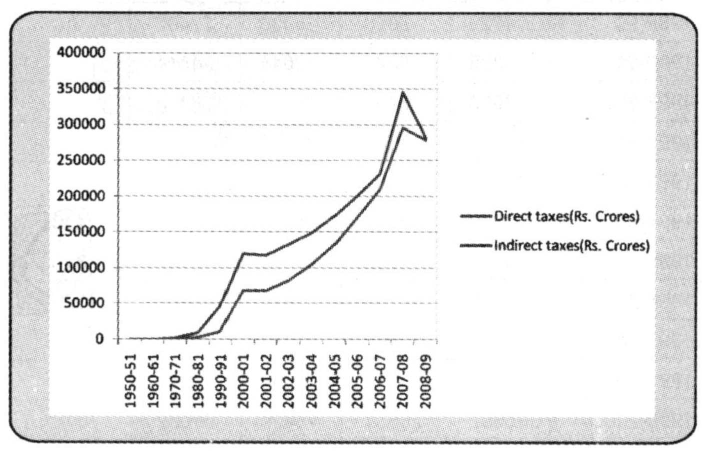

Fig. 3.1

Source: Compiled from Public Finance, CMIE Publication, November 2006, Economic Survey 2008-09

Table 3.5: Gross Tax Revenue of the Central Government

(Rs. Crores)

Financial year	Corpoation tax	Income tax	Custom duty	Exicse duty	Service tax
1	2	3	4	5	6
1979-80	1392	1340	2924	6011	-
1980-81	1377	1440	3409	6500	-
1981-82	1970	1476	4300	7421	-
1982-83	2185	1570	5119	8059	-
1983-84	2493	1699	5583	10222	-
1984-85	2556	1928	7041	11151	-
1985-86	2865	2511	9526	12956	-
1986-87	3160	2879	11475	14470	-
1987-88	3433	3192	13702	16426	-

(Contd...)

1	2	3	4	5	6
1988-89	4407	4241	15805	18841	-
1989-90	4729	5010	18036	22406	-
1990-91	5335	5371	20644	24514	-
1991-92	7853	6731	22257	28110	-
1992-93	8899	7888	23776	30832	-
1993-94	10060	9123	22193	31697	-
1994-95	13822	12025	26789	37347	410
1995-96	16487	15592	35757	40187	846
1996-97	18567	18231	42851	45008	1022
1997-98	20016	17097	40193	47962	1515
1998-99	24529	20240	40668	53246	1787
1999-2000	30692	25654	48420	61902	2072
2000-01	35696	31764	47542	68526	2540
2001-02	36609	32004	40268	72555	3305
2002-03	46172	36866	44852	82310	4125
2003-04	63562	41387	48629	90774	7890
2004-05	82680	49259	57611	99125	14196
2005-06	103573	66239	64215	112000	23053
2006-07	133010	77409	77066	119000	38169
2007-08	192911	102644	104119	123611	50603
2008-09(R.E.)	122600	222000	108000	108359	65000

Source: Compiled from Public Finance, CMIE Publication, November 2006, Economic Survey 2008-09

Table 3.6: Gross Tax Revenue of the Central Government

(Percentage of Gross Tax Revenue)

Financial year	Corpoation tax	Income tax	Custom duty	Exicse duty	Service tax
1	2	3	4	5	6
1979-80	11.59	11.15	24.35	50.04	-
1980-81	10.47	10.95	25.93	49.43	-

(Contd...)

1	2	3	4	5	6
1981-82	12.46	9.33	27.19	46.92	-
1982-83	12.35	8.87	28.93	45.54	-
1983-84	12.03	8.02	26.94	49.33	-
1984-85	10.89	8.21	30.00	47.51	-
1985-86	9.99	8.76	33.23	45.19	-
1986-87	9.62	8.77	34.94	44.06	-
1987-88	9.11	8.47	36.38	43.61	-
1988-89	9.91	9.54	35.54	42.36	-
1989-90	9.16	9.07	34.93	43.39	-
1990-91	9.27	9.33	35.86	42.58	-
1991-92	11.66	9.99	33.04	41.73	-
1992-93	11.92	10.57	31.86	41.31	-
1993-94	13.28	12.04	29.03	41.85	-
1994-95	14.98	13.03	29.03	40.47	0.44
1995-96	14.82	14.02	32.15	36.13	0.78
1996-97	14.42	14.16	33.28	34.95	0.82
1997-98	14.38	12.28	28.87	34.45	1.14
1998-99	17.06	14.08	28.28	37.03	1.36
1999-00	17.87	14.94	28.19	36.04	1.24
2000-01	18.93	16.84	25.21	36.33	1.39
2001-02	19.57	17.11	21.53	38.79	1.77
2002-03	21.35	17.05	20.74	38.06	1.91
2003-04	24.99	16.27	19.12	35.69	3.01
2004-05	27.11	16.15	18.89	32.05	4.66
2005-06	27.98	17.09	17.35	30.26	6.21
2006-07	30.08	17.51	18.02	26.91	7.08
2007-08	32.05	17.03	17.06	20.08	8.06
2008-09 (R.E.)	35.04	19.05	17.02	17.03	10.4

Source: Compiled from Public Finance, CMIE Publication, November 2006, Economic Survey 2008-09

Table 3.5 and3.6 depicts the revenue collection and percentage of gross tax revenue of the five major taxes of the Central Government. Different taxes shows quite distinct time profiles. In 1979-80 Excise duty was the major revenue contributor with Rs. 6011 crores revenue and accounted for 50.04 per cent of tax revenue that clearly indicates the dominance of manufacturing sector over the other. Customs Duty contributes Rs. 2924 crores and it was accounted for 24.35 per cent of the total gross tax revenue in the year 1979-80. The share of corporation and income tax were Rs.1392 crores and Rs. 1340 crores respectively and accounted for 11.59 per cent and 11.15 per cent of gross tax revenue. The trend clearly indicates that in 1979-80 the contribution of indirect taxes are much more than direct axes. The share of Excise Duty continuously decline it was decreased to 42.36 per cent in 1989-90, to 36.04 per cent in 1999-2000 and 17.3 per cent in 2008-09. The percentage of Custom Duty has been varying it increased to 34.93 in 1989-90 and in the very next decade it shows a declining trend and decreased to 28.19 in 1999-2000 and 17.2 in 2008-09. Both corporation and income tax were showing increasing

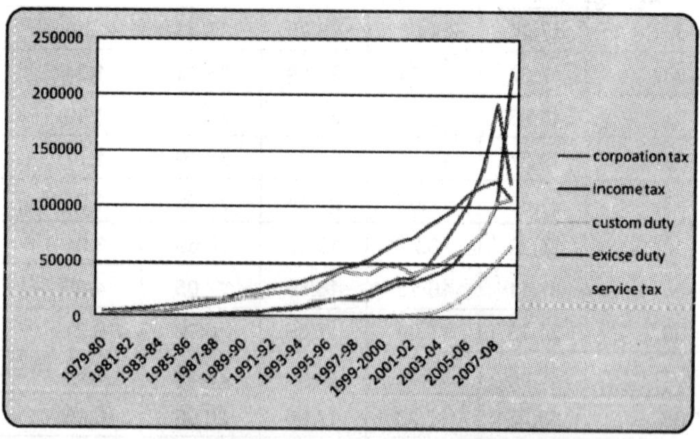

Fig. 3.2 : Gross Tax Revenue of Central Government

Source: Compiled from Public Finance, CMIE Publication, November 2006, Economic Survey 2008-09

trend after the introduction of New Economic Policy in 1991 the share of income tax increased to 12.04 in 1993-94, 14.94 in 1999-2000 to 19.5 in 2008-09. The share of corporation tax was increased to 35.4 per cent in 2008-09 from the meager share of 9.16 in 1989-90. The percentage share of Service Tax also shows the rapid increase from 0.44 per cent in 1994-95 to 10.4 per cent in 2008-09 and indicates that the share of services in the tax revenue is growing very fast. The revenue growth of different taxes can be seen from the Figure 3.2 also.

FUTURE PRESPECTIVE

The future shape of Indian tax structure is moving gradually towards its complete transformation. It is proposed to introduce a Direct Tax Code by deleting a number of taxes and to be replaced by a single tax at the rate of 25 per cent on corporation and individuals above the income of Rs. 25,00,000 lakhs the proposed rate would be 30 per cent which is the maximum limit. All the indirect taxes are to be comprehended within the proposed Goods and Services Tax (GST). In the area of indirect taxes a landmark step was taken through the introduction of VAT in 2005. Though the basic framework of new tax structure direct as well as indirect is clear but the details and the modality of implementation of the new provisions are yet to come to light. The date line fixed for the enforcement of the new tax structure is 1st April 2010.

REFERENCES

1. Substituted by the Constitution (Sixth Amendment) Act,1956.
2. The word 'and advertisements broadcast by radio or television'. Inserted by the Constitution (Forty-Second Amendment) Act, 1976.
3. Inserted by the Constitution (Sixth Amendment) Act, 1956.

4. Inserted by the Constitution (Forty-Sixth Amendment) Act, 1982.
5. Inserted by the Constitution (Eighty-Eighth Amendment) Act, 2003.
6. The Scope of these taxes is spelt out in Article 276, the clause(2) of which fixes the amount payable by a person on account of these taxes.
7. Report of the Tax Reform Committee(1991) constituted under the chairmanship of Dr. Raja J. Chelliah, p. 123.

Service Tax in India

INTRODUCTION

The origin of service as a tax base in modern times might be traced back to Irving Fisher's study on the Nature and Concept of Income. While examining the satisfaction element he opined that income could only be satisfactorily described in terms of consumption or services received. According to his view income "is a flow of services through a period of time."[1] One can easily assumes that the flow of services for example the services of dwelling to its owner (shelter of money rentals), the services of piano (music) and the services of food (nourishment) *etc.* could be used as a tax base and subjected to Service Tax.[2]

Though Fisher was formulating the basis for a broad based concept of income however when he included earning from services rendered as income there is a clear pointer that the service provider may also be considered for levying tax on services rendered. When sales tax was levied the services were negligible and it was considered not administratively feasible to levy tax on services. Further, due to difficulty in measuring the money value of each and every service and complexities in collecting Service Tax were considered not feasible to administer and enforce efficiently.

In spite of several deficiencies in the income, tax on income remained the dominant contributor of direct tax revenue throughout the world. Industrial sector and agricultural sector were continued to get attention in almost all countries. The service sector came to limelight only in the last quarter of the Twentieth Century and it was found most lucrative source of revenue. Presently Service Tax is levied in about 150 countries in different shapes and forms.

In India a paradigm shift has taken place in the year 1991 when policy of mixed economy was replaced by market economy. The trend towards Liberalization, Privatization and Globalization of the economy was initiated in a gradual manner. The public sector is being dismantled through the policy of disinvestment. Within three years of the introduction of the New Economic Policy a humble start was made in the field of Service Tax in the year 1994. Prior to that the growth of service sector was not found suitable for tax purposes. When the Constitution of India was being framed and the taxing power was being distributed between Centre and States the entry of Service Tax was conspicuously absent from the entire three lists. It was only in 2003 that a new entry 92C was added in the Union List only. Thus, the States have no right to impose Service Tax till date under the federal Constitution of India.

ROLE OF SERVICE SECTOR

The service industry forms the backbone of social and economic development of a region. It has emerged as the largest and fastest-growing sectors in the world economy, making higher contributions to the global output and employment. Its growth rate has been higher than that of agriculture and manufacturing sectors. It is a large and most dynamic part of the Indian economy both in terms of employment potential and contribution to national income. It covers a wide range of activities, such as trading, transportation and communication, financial, real estate and business services, as well as community, social and personal services.

Service sector has become important for developing economies throughout the world and is very significant particularly for India. While for the medium and long term targets, it is important to accelerate the growth of industrial sector particularly manufacturing sector to catch up with the growth of service sector. It has also to maintain a high and stable growth of agricultural sector, which is still subject to the vagaries of nature, in the short and even medium term. The sure bet for higher growth of the Indian economy lies in further accelerating the growth of the services sector, which can be done with considerable ease compared to other sectors. This is evident from the following facts and figures. In India, the growth rate of services in 2004-05, 2005-06 and 2006-07 were 9.6 per cent, 9.8 per cent and 11.0 per cent, respectively and is expected to grow at 9.9 per cent in the11th Plan. India is making all its efforts towards increasing its role in global services export from the present its 2.7 per cent share in the global services market to 4-5 per cent in the next 3-4 years. Some new incentives are likely to be extended to the services sector through the coming foreign Trade Policy in September 2009.[3] The growth of service sector is much faster than the growth of industry and agriculture. The share of service sector in GDP is increasing very fast as compared to other sectors. This trend is implicit in the following table 4.1:

The table shows that the contribution of service in GDP is increasing very fast as compared to other sectors. In 1970-71 share of agriculture was 39.37 per cent which decreased to 16.97 per cent in 2006-07. If we look at the industry we

Table 4.1: Sectoral Share of GDP

(In Percentage)

Year	Agriculture	Industry	Services
1970-71	39.37	22.07	33.55
1980-81	34.37	22.04	38.04
1990-91	28.75	25.92	42.71
1991-92	27.69	25.62	44.05
1992-93	28.13	25.12	44.18
1993-94	27.47	25.15	44.84
1994-95	27.04	25.84	44.63
1995-96	24.96	26.87	45.80
1996-97	25.52	26.55	45.62
1997-98	23.74	26.40	47.60
1998-99	23.83	25.77	48.32
1999-2000	22.93	25.31	49.69
2000-01	21.84	25.80	50.31
2001-02	21.97	25.05	50.96
2002-03	19.44	25.82	52.75
2003-04	19.86	25.55	52.73
2004-05	18.47	26.24	53.56
2005-06	17.91	26.42	54.02
2006-07	16.97	26.75	54.74
2007-08	-	26.63	55.62

Source: National Income Statistics, CMIE Publication. (July, 2008)

find that the share is increasing, it increased from 22.07 per cent in 1970-71 to 26.63 per cent in 2007-08. The share of service in GDP is increased from 33.55 per cent in 1970-71 to 55.62 per cent in 2007-08. Thus, service sector is the most lucrative source of public revenue. The growth of service sector can also be evident from the Chart below:

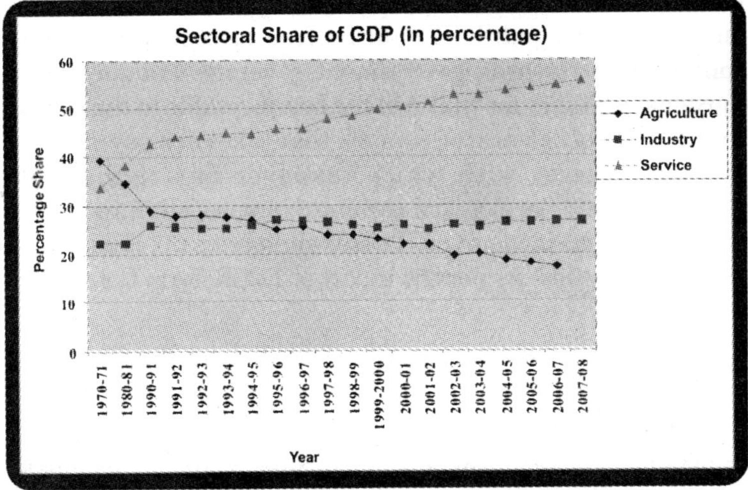

Fig. 4.1

Source: National Income Statistics, CMIE Publication, July 2008

JUSTIFICATION FOR IMPOSING SERVICE TAX

While introducing the Service Tax in the budget 1994-95 speech Dr. Manmohan Singh, then the Union Finance Minister in his speech said:

> Over the years, while attempts have been made to widen the base for domestic indirect taxes, the service sector has not been subject to taxation. Yet this sector accounts for about 40 per cent of our GDP and is showing strong growth. There is no sound reason for exempting services from taxation, when goods are taxed and many countries treat goods and services alike for tax purpose. The Tax Reform Committee has also recommended imposition of tax on services as a measure for tax broadening the base of indirect taxes.[4]

Service sector is a very strong potential source of public revenue. Moreover, while manufacture, distribution (sale) and consumption of goods are taxable, leaving aside the services as free of taxes are not logically justified. No service enjoyed by the public should be free of cost and a small contribution towards government revenues should not be burdensome taxes for that will not be acceptable to the society in the spirit of celebrated remark that taxes are payment for civilized society with which taxpayer buy civilization. Comparatively Service Tax is easy to impose, administer and collect than the income tax. Therefore, service tax is equitable and well justified. As per the report of Tax Reform Committee 1991:

> The substantial broadening of base through the taxation of services would enable the lowering of rates of commodity taxation. A general value added tax levied even at 10 per cent covering imports and domestically produced commodities and services plus a selective excise at a limited number of higher rates on a few commodities should be able to fetch sufficient revenues.[5]

The service sector today encompasses a wide range of activities such as management, banking, insurance, hospitality, administration, communication, entertainment, wholesale distribution and retailing, including research and developmental activities. The growth of service sector is much faster than the growth of industry and agriculture The service sector's contribution to GDP growth has been more than 50 percent since 1997-98. The share of the service sector in GDP is 55 percent in 2007-08.

CONSTITUTIONALITY OF SERVICE TAX

The 88th amendment of the constitution of India in the year 2003 establishes the constitutional basis empowering the Union Government to impose Service Tax. Article 268A provides that taxes on services should be levied by the Government of India and such tax shall be collect and appropriated by the Government of India and the States. In accordance with the other principles laid down by the government. It also amends the List I of the Seventh Schedule which empowers the Central Government to impose tax on services by inserting 92(c). The aforesaid constitutional provision was inserted on the suggestion of Kelkar Committee report, before this cleared provision was added the constitutional validity of the Service Tax was challenged before the courts. Various High Courts and the Supreme Court have upheld the power of Union Government to impose Service Tax under the residuary entry 97.

LEGISLATIVE HISTORY OF SERVICE TAX

The provisions relating to Service Tax were brought into force with effect from 1st July, 1994. A modest effort was made by imposing a tax on services of telephones, non-life insurance and stock brokers. The tax will be charged at 5 percent on the amount of telephone bills, the net premium charged by the insurance companies and the brokerage or commission charged by the stock brokers in relation to their services.

The services, brought under the tax net in the year 1994-95 are explained below:

1. **Telephone:** It includes Director General, Posts and Telegraphs, MTNL, BSNL and other licenced agencies, sale of simcards and activation charges inter connectivity, linked charges. It includes activities of cellular telephone service providers, wireless speech service providers. It did not included e-mail service, internet services, infrastructure charges, port charges at that time.
2. **Stock-Brokers:** Stock broker is a person who has either made an application for registration or is registered as a stock broker in accordance with the rules and regulations made under the Security and Exchange Board of India (SEBI) Act, 1992. It would also include a registered sub-broker.

3. **General Insurance Business:** It included fire, marine or miscellaneous insurance business whether carried out singly or in combination with one or more several activities, but did not include capital redemption business and annuity business.

In the year 1996, the Service Tax net was expanded by including the following services:

1. **Advertising Agency**: It means any commercial concern engaged in providing any service connected with the making, preparation, display or exhibition of advertisement and included an advertisement consultant. Advertisement included any notice, circular, label, wrapper, document, hoarding or any other audio/visual representation made by means of light, sound, smoke or gas.
2. **Courier Agency**: It means a commercial concern engaged in the door to door transportation of time sensitive documents, goods and articles utilizing the services of a person, either directly or indirectly, to carry or accompany such documents, goods and articles.
3. **Pager Service**: It means an instrument, apparatus or appliance which is a non-speech, one way personal calling system with alert and has the capability of receiving, storing and displaying numeric or alpha numeric massages.

In the year 1997, the government has also widened the net of Service Tax by including the following services:

1. **Air Travel Agent:** It means any person engaged in providing any service connected with the booking of passage for travel by air.
2. **Clearing and Forwarding Agent:** It means any person who is engaged in providing any service, either directly or indirectly connected with clearing and forwarding operation in any manner to any other person and includes a consignment agent.

3. **Consulting Engineer:** It means any professionally qualified engineer or an engineering firm who, either directly or indirectly, renders any advice, consultancy or technical assistance in any manner to a client in one or more disciplines of engineering.
4. **Custom House Agent:** It means a person licensed, temporarily or otherwise under the regulation made under sub-section (2) of the section 146 of the Customs Act, 1962.
5. **Goods Transport Operator:** It means any commercial concerns engaged in the transportation of goods but does not include a courier agency.
6. **Mandap Keeper:** It means a person who allows temporary occupation of a mandap for consideration for organizing any official, social or business function. Mandap means any immovable property as defined in section 3 of the transfer of Property Act, 1882 and includes any furniture, fixtures, light fittings and floor covering therein let out for consideration for organizing any official, social or business function.
7. **Manpower Recruitment Agency:** It means any commercial concern engaged in providing any service, directly or indirectly in any manner for recruitment of manpower to a client.
8. **Outdoor Caterer:** It means a caterer engaged in providing services in connection with catering at a place other than his own. Caterer means any person who supplies, either directly or indirectly, any food edible preparations alcoholic or non-alcoholic beverages or crockery and similar articles or accoutrements for any purpose or occasion.
9. **Pandal or Shamiana Contractor:** It means a person engaged in providing any service either directly or indirectly, in connection with the preparation , arrangement , erection or decoration of

a pandal or shamiana and includes the supply of furnitures, fixtures, lights and lighting fittings floor coverings and other articles for use therein.

10. **Rent-a-cab scheme operator :** It means a person who is the holders of a licence under the Rent-a-cab scheme 1989, framed by the central Government under the Motor Vehicles Act , 1988 cab means motor cab or maxi cab.
11. **Steamer Agent:** It means any person who undertakes, either directly or indirectly (*a*) to perform any service in connection with the ship's husbandry or dispatch including the rendering of administrative work related thereto; or (*b*) to book, advertise or canvass for cargo for or on behalf of a shipping line; or (*c*) to provide container feeder services for or on behalf of a shipping line.
12. **Tour Operator:** It means any person engaged in the business of operating tour in tourist vehicle covered by a permit granted under the Motor Vehicles Act, 1988 or the rules made there under.

The service provided by goods transport operators, outdoor caterers and pandal or shamiana contractors were brought under the tax net in the budget 1997-98 but abolished vide Notification No. 49/98, 2nd June 1998.

Government of India has notified imposition of service tax on twelve new services in the year 1998.They are as below:

1. **Architect:** It means any person whose name is for the time being, entered in the register of architects maintained under section 23 of the Architect Act, 1972 and also includes any commercial concern engaged in any manner, whether directly or indirectly in rendering services in the field of architecture.
2. **Credit Rating Agency:** It means any commercial concern engaged in the business of credit rating of

any debt obligation or of any project or programme requiring finance whether in the form of debt or otherwise and includes credit rating of any purpose of providing a potential investor or any other person any information pertaining to the relative safety of timely payment of interest or principal.

3. **Interior Decorator:** It means any person engaged whether directly or indirectly in the business of providing by way of advice, consultancy, technical assistance or in any other manner, service related to planning , design or beatification of spaces, whether man made or otherwise and includes a landscape designer.

4. **Management Consultant:** It means any person who is engaged in providing any service either directly or indirectly in connection with the management of any organization in any manner and includes any person who renders any advice, consultancy or technical assistance, relating to conceptualizing, devising development , modification rectification or up gradation of any working system of any organization.

5. **Market Research Agency:** It means any commercial concern engaged in conducting market research in any manner, in relation to any product, service or utility including all types of customized and syndicated research service.

6. **Merchandised Slaughter Home:** It means a commercial concern engaged in the business of slaughtering of animals with the aid of machine.

7. **Practising Chartered Accountants:** It means a person who is a member of the institute of Chartered Accountants of India and is holding a certificate of Practice granted under the provision of the Chartered Accountant Act 1949 and includes any concern

engaged in rendering services in the field of chartered accountancy.

8. **Practicing Cost Accountant:** It means a person who is a member of the Institute of Cost and Works Accountants of India and is holding a certificate of practice granted under the provision of the Cost and Works Accountants Act 1959 and includes any concerns engaged in rendering service in the field of cost accountancy.

9. **Practicing Company Secretary:** It means a person who is a member of the Institute of Company Secretaries of India and is holding a certificate of practice granted under the provision of the Company Secretaries Act 1980 and includes any concern engaged in rendering services in the field of company secretaryship.

10. **Real Estate Agent and Real Estate Consultant:** It means a person who is engaged in rendering any service in relation to sale, purchase, leasing or renting of real estate and includes a real estate consultant. Real Estate Consultant means a person who renders in any manner either directly or indirectly advice, consultancy or technical assistance, in relation to evaluation, conception, design, development, construction implementation, supervision, maintenance, marketing acquisition or management of real estate.

11. **Private Security Services:** It means any commercial concern engaged in the business of rendering the services relating to the security of any property, whether movable or immovable or of any person, in any manner and include the service of investigation, detection or verification of any fact or activity whether of a personal nature or otherwise including the services of providing security personnel.

12. **Under Writing Agencies:** It has the meaning assigned to it in clause (g) of rule 2 of the Securities and Exchange Board of India (under writers) Rules 1993.

In case of mechanized slaughter houses, since exempted vide Notification No. 58/98 dated 07-10-98.

In the year 1999, the Government did not add any service under tax net and make no amendment and substitution of any provision of the Act. In the year 2000 the Government did not expand the Service Tax net. By Finance Bill 2000, some amendments in section 66, 65 and 67 had been proposed , but unfortunately this was not materialized. The Hon'ble Finance Minister announced the constitution of an Expert Group to study the entire gamut of issues relating to Service Tax in his budget speech in Lok Sabha on 29-02-2000. The Finance Minister in his budget speech said:

> Service Tax is emerging as area of promise as well as problems. Many experts advice me that the best way to deal with this tax is to make it applicable to all services in one go. However, some other has suggested basic changes in the very structure of Service Tax. I have decided not to make any changes for the present. I am setting up an Expert Group to go into all aspects of the matter, review the experience so far, and give me its considered advice.[6]

According the Government constituted seven members in Expert Group under the chairmanship of Dr. M. Govinda Rao. Terms of reference of Expert Group are following:

(*i*) To examine the existing structure of Service Tax and make recommendation on extending the tax base in the areas of services and the timing thereof;

(*ii*) To examine the procedure for collection of Service Tax and to make recommendation as may be considered necessary for making it more effective to augment voluntary compliance and to reduce compliance cost.

(*iii*) To make recommendation on any other matter related to the above points or incidental thereto.

In interim Report, the Expert Group has addressed the issues of immediate relevance that need to be addressed in the forthcoming budget. These includes the matters related to extension of coverage under the Service Tax, approach and strategy that should be adopted to extend the tax base on services , items of services that should be exempted from the purview of taxation and the development of administrative organization for scientific administration and enforcement of the tax. The deliberation of Expert Group were spread over a period of several months i.e. July 2000 to March 2001 and ultimately after an elaborate discussion on Interim Report was submitted in Nov. 2000 with a view to assist the Government in finalizing the Service Tax. The Final Report containing recommendations on *inter alia* 11 major issues *inter alia* was submitted on 30th March 2001 as follows:

1. A separate, self enactment on Service Tax should be legislated to administer the Service Tax.
2. Certain services which are developmental in nature in cater to primarily lower strata of society, may be exempted for limited period.
3. The unorganized sector and small service providers should be kept out of the purview of this tax by prescribing a threshold exemption limit of annual turnover up to Rs. 10 Lakhs.
4. The service sector should be comprehensively covered under the service tax net. However services relating to utilities, sovereign functions of the state, essential health and education services could be excluded from the Service Tax net by incorporating a well define negative list.

5. The rate of Service Tax for the present could be retained at the present moderate rate of 5 percent.
6. In the mean time, the input credit should be immediately allowed with the service sector. Inter-sectoral credits between goods and services could be extended along with integration into CENVAT.
7. The tax on services should be eventually integrated with Central Excise Duties on goods to evolve into a comprehensive CENVAT on goods and services by 2004-05.
8. An improved administrative arrangement with increased financial autonomy is important for successful implementation of this tax.
9. In order to facilitate voluntary tax compliance and to cut down taxpayer inconveniencies the Service Tax should be administer as a first e-tax of the country with self assessment and risk based audit and on line web based connectivity with assesses.
10. The Central Government should consider sharing of powers to tax services with the states once the latter are committed to uniformly introduce comprehensive destination.
11. A well-orchestrated publicity campaign for taxpayer education is essential for smooth implementation of our recommendation.

In the year 2001, the government pursuing the recommendation of Expert Committee, widened the scope of tax by including fourteen services under the tax net. They are as follows:

1. **Banking and other Financial Services:** It means the following services provided by a banking company or a financial institution including a non-banking financial company namely:
   (*i*) Financial leasing services including equipment leasing and higher purchase by a body corporate.

(*ii*) Credit and services

(*iii*) Merchant banking services

(*iv*) Securities and foreign exchange (Forex)

(*v*) Assets management including portfolio management all forms of funnel management, pension fund management, custodial depository and trust services but does not includes cash management.

(*vi*) Advisory and other auxiliary financial services including investment and portfolio research and advice, advice on mergers and acquisitions and advice on corporate restructuring and strategy.

(*vii*) Provision and transfer of information and data processing.

2. **Broadcasting:** It has the meaning assigned to it in clause (c) of section 2 of the Prasar Bharti (Broadcasting Corporation of India) Act, 1990. As per section 2(c) of the Prasar Bharti Act 1990, 'Broadcasting' meaning the dissemination of any form of communication like signs, signals, writing, pictures, images and sounds of all kinds by transmission of electromagnetic waves through apace or through cables intended to be received by the general public either directly or indirectly through the medium of relay station and all its grammatical variations and cognate expressions shall be construed accordingly.

3. **Convention:** It means a formal meeting or assembly which is not open to the general public and does not includes a meeting or assembly the principal any type of amusement, entertainment or recreation.

4. **Facsimile(FAX):** It means a form of telecommunication by which fixed graphic images, such as printed texts and pictures are scanned and the information converted into electrical signals for transmission over the telecommunication system.

5. **Insurance Auxiliary Services:** It means any service provided by an actuary, an intermediary or insurance agent in relation to general insurance business and includes risk assessment, claim settlement, survey and loss assessment.
6. **On Line information and Database Access or Retrieval:** It means providing data or information, retrievable or otherwise, to customer in electronic form through a computer network. This definition will undergo a change by replacing 'to any person' in place of 'to a client' as proposed in a Finance Bills, 2008.
7. **Photography:** It includes still photography, Motion pictures photography, laser photography, aerial photography and fluorescent photography.
8. **Port Services:** It means any services rendered by a port or any person authorized by the port, in any manner, in relation to a vessel or goods.
9. **Scientific and Technical Consultancy:** It means any advice, consultancy or scientific or technical assistance rendered in any manner, either directly or indirectly by a scientist or technocrat or any science or technology institution or organization, to a client, in one or more disciplines of science or technology.
10. **Sound Recording:** It means recording of sound on a magnetic storage device and editing thereof in any manner.
11. **Telegraph:** It has the meaning assigned to it in clause (i) of section 3 of the Indian Telegraph Act 1885. According to it Telegraph means any appliance, instruments, material or apparatus used or capable of used for transmission or reception of signs, signals, writing, images and sounds or intelligence of any nature by wire, visual or other electro-magnetic emissions, Radio waves or Hertzain waves, galvanic, electric or magnetic means.

12. **Telex:** It means a typed communication by using teleprompters through telex exchange.
13. **Vide Tape Production:** It means the process of any recording of any programme, even to or functions on a magnetic tape and includes editing thereof, in any manner.
14. **Authorized Service Stations:** It means any service station or centre, authorized by any motor vehicle manufacturer, to carry out any service or repair of any motor car or two wheeler motor vehicle manufactured by such manufacturer.
15. **Leased Circuit Services:** It means a dedicated link provided between two fired locations for exclusive use of subscriber and includes speech circuit, data circuit or a telegraph circuit.

In the year 2002 the Finance Minister in his present budget speech has proposed the following new services:

1. **Beauty Parlours:** It means any establishment providing beauty treatment service. 'Beauty Treatment' means face and beauty treatment, osmetic treatment, manicure, pedicure or counselling rvices or beauty face care or make-up.

Cable Operator: It shall have the meaning assigned to it in clause(a) of Section 2 of the Cable Television Networks(regulation) Act, 1995. According to it cable service through a cable television network or otherwise controls or is responsible for the management and operation of a cable television network.

3. **Cargo Handling Service:** It means loading, unloading, packing or unpacking of cargo and includes cargo handling services provided for freight in special containers or for non-containerized freight, services provided by container freight terminal or any other freight terminal, for all modes of transport and

cargo handling services, incidental to freight, but does not include handling of export cargo or passenger baggage or mere transportation of goods.

4. **Dry Cleaning:** It includes dry cleaning of apparel, garments or other textile fur or leather articles.
5. **Event Management:** It means any service provided in relation to planning, promotion, organizing or presentation of any arts, entertainment, business, sports or any other event and includes any consultation provided in this regard.
6. **Fashion Designing:** It include any activity relating to conceptualizing, outlining, creating the designs and preparing pattern for customers, apparels, garments, clothing, accessories, jewelry or any other articles intended to be worn by human beings and any other service incidental thereto.
7. **Health and Fitness Services:** It means service for physical well-being such as sauna and stem bath, Turkish bath, solarium spas, reducing or slimming salons, gymnasium, yoga, meditation, message (excluding therapeutic massage) or any other like service.
8. **Life Insurance Auxiliary Service:** It means any service provided by an actuary, an intermediary or insurance intermediary or an insurance agent in relation to general insurance business or life insurance business and includes risk assessment, claim settlement, survey and loss assessment.
9. **Rail Travel Agent:** It means any person engaged in providing any service connected with booking of passage for travel by air.
10. **Storage and Warehousing:** It includes storage and warehousing service for goods including liquids and gases but does not include any service provided for storage of agriculture produce or any service by a cold storage.

In the year 2003, the levy of service tax has been extended to following new services:

1. **Commercial vocational institutions, coaching centers, private tuitions:** It includes institutions providing commercial coaching or Training, coaching classes, tutorials classes, motor driving classes, beauty and working classes etc. and does not include Sports training, pre-school coaching centers, institutions giving degree/diploma, individuals tuitions at home, hobby, vocational and computer classes.
2. **Technical testing and analysis (excluding health and diagnostic testing) technical inspection and certification services :** It includes testing analysis, inspection, certification, inspection/ examination of goods / processes / material property, standard testing, chemical testing and it exclude health and diagnostic testing, pollution testing, environmental tests, whether forecasts, test on humans and animals.
3. **Maintenance and repair services:** it include commercial repair, maintenance, service under agreement or contract, repair etc. of goods or equipment by manufacturer, authorized repair service.
4. **Commission and installation services:** It includes commissioning / installation of projects, equipments, plant and machinery and does not includes consulting engineer's services, repair and maintenance.
5. **Business auxiliary services:** It means business promotion and support services, processes out sourcing, customer care, managing front offices, launching of products, customer education programme, Seminars, data warehousing help desk services, enquiry bureaus, housekeeping, accounts,

computer enabled services, data processing, networking, back office processing, computer facility management, call centres, medical transcription centers.

6. **Internet cafe:** Internet access services sale of internet hours and it does not include other services provided by Internet café / Kiosks call centres etc. computer job work.
7. **Franchise Services:** it means franchisee fee, royalty, other fees by whatever name called and it will not take franchisee providing other services not related to franchiser.

In the year 2003-04 Budget the rate of Service Tax was increased from five per cent to eight per cent on all the taxable services.

The budgets 2004-05, 10, are services have been introduced in the service tax net along with the reintroduction of three existing services. They are as follows:

1. **Business Exhibition Services:** It means an exhibition to market or to promote or to advertise or to showcase any product or service, intended for the growth in business of the producer or provider of such product or service, as the case may be. It will not include the services of event management and advertising services.
2. **Airport Services:** It includes services provided to any person by airport authority or any person authorized by it an airport or a civil enclave.
3. **Transport of Goods by Air Services:** It includes services rendered to any person by an aircraft operator, in relation to transport of goods by aircraft.
4. **Minerals survey and exploration services:** It includes services rendered to customer, by any person in relation of minerals. As per section 65(104 A) survey and exploration of minerals means geological,

geophysical or other prospecting, surface of subsurface surveying or map making services in relation to location or exploration of deposits of mineral, oil or gas.

5. **Opinion Poll Services:** It includes services rendered to any person by an opinion poll agency in relation to opinion poll. As per section 65(75 A), opinion poll means any service designed to secure information on public opinion regarding social, economic, political or other issues.

6. **Intellectual Property Services:** It includes service provided to any person by the holder of intellectual property right, in relation to intellectual property services.

7. **Forward Contract Services:** It includes services rendered to any person by a member of a recognized association or any registered association in relation to a forward contract.

8. **TV and Radio Production services:** It includes services rendered to person by a programme producer, in relation to a programme producer, in relation to a programme. As per section 65(86 B), a programme producer means any person who producers a programme on behalf of another person.

9. **Construction Services:** It includes services rendered to any person, by a commercial concern in relation to commercial concern in relation to commercial or industrial construction service.

10. **Travel Agent (other than Air/Rail Travel) Services:** It includes services rendered to a customer by a travel agent in relation to the booking of passage free travel.

11. **Pandal and Shamiana Services (Reintroduced)** : These services were brought under service tax vide Finance Act, 1997 followed by Notification No. 28/97

dated 25-7-1997, however , subsequently discounted w.e.f. 2-6-1998. The Finance Act, 2004 has reintroduced service tax on Pandal and Shamiana Services.

Services provided to a client by a pandal or shamiana contractor in relation to a pandal or shamiana in any manner and also includes the services, if any, provided or to be provided as a caterer.

In the Budget 2005-06, 9 more services have been introduced in the service tax net as follows with effect from 16-06-05.

1. **Transport Services through Pipeline or conduit:** It includes transport services to any person, by any other person, in relation to transport of goods other than water, through pipeline or other conduit.
2. **Site Formation Services:** It includes services provided to any person, by any other person, in relation to site formation and clearance, excavation and earthmoving demolition and such other similar activities.
3. **Dredging Services:** It includes services provided to any person, by any other person, in relation to dredging of rivers, port, harbors, backwater and estuaries.
4. **Survey and map making:** It includes services provided to any person, by any other person, other than by an agency under the control of, or authorized by, the Government, in relation to survey and map making.
5. **Cleaning Services:** It includes services provided to any person, in relation to cleaning activity. It means cleaning, including specialized cleaning services such as, disinfecting, exterminating or sterilizing of objects or premises, of:

(*i*) Commercial or industrial building and premises thereof; or

(*ii*) Factory, plant or machinery, tank or reservoir of such commercial or industrial buildings and premises thereof, but does not include such services in relation to agriculture horticulture, animal husbandry or dairying.

6. **Membership of Clubs and Association Services:** It includes services provided to its members, by any club or association in relation to provision of services, facilities or advantages for a subscription or any other amount.

7. **Packaging Services :** It includes services provided to any person, by other person, in relation to packaging activity it means packaging of goods including pouch filling, bottling, labeling or imprinting of the package, but does not include any packaging activity that amounts to 'manufacture' within the meaning of clause (f) of section 2 of the Central Excise Act, 1944.

8. **Mailing Services:** It includes services provided to any person, in relation to mailing list compilation and mailing.

9. **Construction of Residential Complex Service :** It includes services provided to any person by any other person, in relation to construction of complex.

In the Budget 2006-07, 15 more services have been introduced in the Service Tax net as follows:

1. **Automated Teller Machine Operations, Maintenance or Management Services:** Certain services provided in relation to ATMs including site selection, contracting of location, value added services etc.

2. **Auctioneer's Service:** Auctioneer's service provided by any person to another person in relation to auction of property which may be movable or immovable, tangible or intangible.
3. **Business Support Services:** Support services also known as back office services, which are outsourced and provided in relation to business or commerce.
4. **Credit Card, Debit Card, Charge Card or other payment card service:** Services in relation to credit cards, debit cards, charge cards, othe payment card services provided by a banking company, financial institution including NBFC or any other person.
5. **Internet Telephony Services:** means Telecommunication service provided through the internet including fax, audio conferencing and video conferencing.
6. **Public Relation Management Services:** Services rendered by agencies managing public relations e.g. strategic counselling, brand launches, press conference and releases etc.
7. **Recovery Agents Services:** Services provided by recovery agents for speedy and timely recovery of loans and amount for sale of a product.
8. **Registrar to an Issue's Service :** Services provided by registrar to an issue including collecting application forms from investors, keeping records pertaining to the issue, finalizing list of persons to whom shares will be allotted.
9. **Share Transfer Agent's Service:** Service provided by any person who maintains the records of holders of securities and deals with all matters connected with the transfer or redemption of securities or activities incidental thereto.
10. **Ship Management Services:** Services relating to operating of ships provided by person engaged in the managing of ships.

11. **Sponsorship Services:** Services relating to naming the event after the sponsor, display of trading name or company's logo, exclusive or priority booking rights, sponsoring prizes trophies for competition etc. However, it does not include services in relation to sponsorship of sports events.
12. **Transport of Goods in Containers by Rail Service:** Service Tax to bne levied on transport of goods in continers by rail from ports to inland container depots and vice versa. However, services provided by Government railways are not subject to Service Tax.
13. **Transport of Passengers Embarking in India for International Journey by Air Service:** Transport of passenger by aircraft oprator where such passenger embarks in India on an international journey.
14. **Transport of Persons Embarking from Port in India by Cruise Ship Service :** It includes transportation of persons embarking from port in India by cruise ship.
15. **Sale of Space or Time for Advertisement Services:** sale of space or time for advertisement excluding sale of space for advertisement in print media as well as time slots by broadcasting agency.

Besides these new services, In this year's budget scope of certain services also expanded.

In the year 2007, Government decided to undertake review of all such circulars, instructions and clarification issued on matters relating to levy and collection of Service Tax, keeping in view the change in Service Tax law, the court pronouncements and other material considerations. For this purpose, government has asked Shri T. R. Rustagi, Chief Commissioner (Retd.) to undertake the aforesaid review and to make recommendations in this behalf to the government.

He has submitted his report to the government on 22-02-2007. As per his report, circulars, instructions and clarification are segregated into the following three categories:

1. To be withdrawn (Annexure A)
2. To be modified (Annexure B)
3. To be retained (Annexure C)

In the Budget of 2007-08, seven new services were brought under the tax net, they are as follows:

1. **Telecommunications Services:** This service nearly merge certain taxable services which are already existing *viz.* telephone service, pager service, leased circuit service, telegraph service, telex service, facsimile(FAX) service.
2. **Design Service:** It means services provided in relation to designing of furniture, consumer products, industrial products, packages, logos, graphics, websites and corporate identity designing and production of three dimensional models.
3. **Mining Service:** It means services for extraction of minerals, oil and gas.
4. **Renting of Immovable Property Service:** It includes renting, letting, leasing, licensing or other similar arrangement of immovable property for use in furtherance of business or commerce but excluding such activity for or by religious body or to an educational body.
5. **Works Contract Services:** it includes service provided or to be provided to any person, by any other person in relation to the execution of a works contract, excluding works contract in respect of roads, airports, railways, transport terminals, bridges, tunnels and dams.

6. **Asset Management Service:** it includes service in relation to asset management including portfolio management and all forms of fund management.
7. **Content Development and Supply Service:** it includes development and supply of mobile value added services, music, movie clips, ringtones, wall papers, mobile games, data, whether or not aggregated, information, news and animation films.

In the year 2008-09 budget these services were brought under the service tax net:

1. **Information Technology Software Service:** It means any representation of instructions, data, sound or image, including source code and object code, recorded in a machine in readable form, and capable of being manipulated or providing interactive to a user, by means of a computer or automatic data processing machine or any other device or equipment.
2. **Investment Management Service Provided under ULIP:** It includes service provided in relation management of investment, known as segregated fund, under unit linked life insurance business.
3. **Stock Exchange, Commodity Exchange and Processing and Clearing House Service:** It includes services provided in relation to recognized stock exchange, recognized or registered association and processing clearing, and settlement of transaction in securities, goods or forward contract.
4. **Sale of Tangible Goods Service:** It includes services providing to any person by any other person in relation to supply of intangible goods including machinery, equipment and appliances for use without transferring right of possession and effective control of such machinery, equipment and appliances.

In the Interim Budget 2009-10 the scope of the tax has not been widened but the rate has been reduced to 10 per cent from 12 per cent.

In the Budget 2009-10 four new services were brought under the tax net. They are as follows:

1. Services provided in relation to transport of goods by rail;
2. Services provided in relation to transport of (*i*) coastal goods; (*ii*) goods through Inland Water including National Waterways;
3. Legal consultancy service; and
4. Cosmetic and plastic surgery service.

In the budget 2010-11 rate of tax on services retained at 10 per cent to pave the way forward for GST. Some of the services were also brought under the tax net they are as follows:

- Service of Promoting, marketing or organizing of games of chance, including lottery
- Health services, namely—Health check-up undertaken by hospitals or medical establishments for the employees of business entities and Health services provided under health insurance schemes offered by insurance companies
- Services provided for maintenance of medical records of employees of a business entity
- Services of promoting of a 'brand' of goods, services, events, business entity etc.
- Services of permitting commercial use or exploitation of any event organized by a person or organization
- Services provided by Electricity Exchanges
- Services related to two types of copyrights hitherto not covered under existing taxable service 'Intellectual Property Right (IPR)', namely, those on (*a*) cinematographic films and (*b*) sound recording
- Special services provided by a builder etc. to the prospective buyers such as providing preferential location or external or internal development of complexes on extra charges.

In this budget the scope of the following services were also expanded. They are as follows:

(1) 'Air Passenger Transport Service' is being expanded to *include* domestic journeys, and international journeys in *any class*.

(2) Presently the taxable service, 'Information Technology Software Service' is subjected to tax only in cases where such IT software is used for furtherance of business or commerce. The scope of the taxable service is being *expanded* to tax such service even if the service provided is used for purposes *other than business or commerce.*

(3) 'Commercial Training or Coaching Service' shall mean that such training or coaching is being provided for a consideration, whether or not such training or coaching is conducted with a profit motive. This change is being given *retrospective effect* from 01.07.2003.

(4) In the definition of the taxable service 'Sponsorship Service' the *exclusion* relating to sponsorship *pertaining to sports* is being removed.

(5) In the definition of the taxable services 'Construction of Complex service' and 'Commercial or industrial construction service' it is being provided that *unless the entire consideration* for the property is *paid after the completion* of construction (i.e. after issuance of completion certificate by the competent authority), the activity of construction would be deemed to be a taxable service provided by the builder / promoter / developer to the prospective buyer and the Service Tax would be charged accordingly.

(6) 'Renting of immovable property'—(*i*) provide explicitly that the activity of 'renting' itself is a taxable service. This change is being given *retrospective effect* from 01.06.2007 and (*ii*) provide that *renting of vacant land*, where the agreement or contract between the

lessor and lessee provides for undertaking construction of buildings or structures on such land for furtherance of business or commerce during the tenure of the lease, shall be subjected to Service Tax.

(7) All *services* provided entirely *within the airport/ port* premises would fall under the 'Airport Services', the 'Port Services' and the 'Other Port Services'; and an authorization from the airport / port authority *not a precondition* for taxing these services.

(8) Auctioneer's Service—Expansion of phrase—'auction by government' means an auction involving sale of *government property* by any auctioneer and *not when the government acts as an auctioneer* for sale of the private property.

(9) 'Management of Investment under ULIP Service'—the *value* of the taxable service for any year of the operation of policy shall be *higher of* the actual amount charged by the insurer *or* the maximum amount of fund management charges fixed by the Insurance Regulatory and Development Authority (IRDA).

RATE STRUCTURE

The rates of Service Tax have been changed from time to time by suitable amendments made in the Finance act, 1994. Through the Finance Act 2003, 2006, 2007 and 2009 as shown in the following table:

Table 4.2: Rate Structure of Service Tax

(In Percentage)

Period	Rate of Service Tax	Effective Rate of Service Tax
1	2	3
w.e.f. 1.7.1994 to 13.5.2003	5	5
w.e.f. 14.5.2003 to 9.9.2004	8	8

1	2	3
w.e.f. 10.9.2004 to 17.4.2006	10 + 2[1]	10.20
w.e.f. 18.4.2006 to 10.5.2007	12 + 2	12.24
w.e.f. 11.5.2007 to 23.2.2009	12 + 2 + 1[2]	12.36
w.e.f. 24.02.2009 to till now	10 + 2 + 1	10.30

Source: Various years Economic Survey and budget Document.

REGISTRATION

Administration of Service Tax is under Central Excise Department. A person liable for Service Tax has to register with Superintendent of Central Excise under whose jurisdiction where the service premises rendering fall. He should register within 30 days from date of commencement of the business of providing taxable service. The person will have to apply for registration (in Form ST-1) Applicant should submit following document at the time of filing application for registration : (*a*) a copy of PAN, (*b*) proof of residence, (*c*) constitution of applicant.

Where an assessee is providing a taxable service from more than one premises or offices and has a centralized billing system or centralized accounting system in respect of such service and such centralized billing or centralized accounting are located in one or more offices or premises, he can register such premises or offices from where centralized billing or centralized accounting system are located. However, where an assessee is providing a taxable service from more than one premises or offices and does not have any centralized billing system, he shall be required to make separate applications for registration in respect of each such premises

[1]Education cess on the amount of Service Tax.

[2]Addition higher education cess on the amount.

or offices to concerned Central Excise Officer under whose jurisdiction it comes.

Where an assessee is providing more than one taxable service, he may make a single application, mentioning therein all the taxable service provided by him to the concerned Central Excise Officer. In other words, only a single registration for all the taxable services provided by the service provider shall be given and the declaration submitted at the time of registration in the application of registration shall be accepted by the jurisdictional Superintendent of Central Excise and the registration must be given immediately but within seven days in any case.

In case of non-resident Indian or a person who was from outside India, who did not have any office in India, registration was not required if he paid the tax under rule 6.

Where a registered assesses transfer his business to another person, the transferee shall obtain a fresh certificate of registration. In other words, certificate of registration is personal to the service provider so long as he continues to carry on business. Once he ceases to be a service provider, the successor is not entitled to carry on the business unless he applies for a registration.

If there is delay, interest for delayed payment will have to be paid, which cannot be waived. Though there is no mandatory penalty for delay in registration, penalty up to Rs 1,000 can be imposed under section 77. In addition, penalty of Rs. 100 per day can be imposed for late payment of tax under section 76. In case of Superintendent of facts, willful mis-statement, fraud and collusion, higher penalty is payable under section 78. The penalty under section 77,78,76 is not automatic. If an assessee proves that there was reasonable cause for delay in registration or payment of Service Tax, the penalty can be waived. However, interest under section 75 for late payment of Service Tax is automatic and it cannot be waived.

PAYMENT OF TAX

Every person providing taxable service to any person shall pay Service Tax as the rate specified in section 66 in such manner and within such period as may be prescribed. The following are the rule for payment of Service Tax.

Due Date for Payment: In case of individual and firm the Service Tax is payable on the value of taxable services received during any quarter. It shall be paid to the credit of the Central Government by the 5th of the month immediately following the quarter towards the value of taxable service. In Case of Others the Service Tax on the value of taxable services received during any calendar month immediately following the calendar month towards the value of taxable services.

Manner and Mode of Payment: The assessee shall deposit the Service Tax liable to be paid by him with the bank designated by the Central Board of Excise and Customs for this purpose in Form TR-6 or in any other manner prescribed by the Central Board of Excise and Customs. However, the assessee who has paid Service Tax of Rs. 50 lacks or above in the preceding financial year or has already paid Service Tax of Rs. 50 lacks in the current financial year, shall deposit the Service Tax liable to be paid by him electronically through internet banking. The following clarifications are also made with regard with regard to e-payment:

- If a person providing taxable services from more than one premises and each premises is separately registered, the criterion of Rs. 50 lakhs would apply to each registered premises individually, as each registered premises is separately an assessee in term of law.
- If a person pays Service Tax from a registered premises for both the taxable services provided by him and the taxable services received by him on

which he is liable to pay Service Tax, the cumulative Service Tax paid, *i.e.* Service Tax paid on taxable service provided from and Service Tax paid on taxable service received in such registered premises would be taken into account for the purpose of satisfaction of criterion of payment of Service Tax amount of Rs. 50 lakh.

- For the purposes of calculation of this amount of Rs. 50 lakh the total Service Tax paid by cash plus CENVAT credit would be taken into account as Service Tax paid amount. Therefore, if an assessee has paid Service Tax of Rs. 50 lakh in cash plus CENVAT credit, such assessee, if he pays any further Service Tax in cash would be required to make mandatory e-payment.

It should be noted that for payment of Service Tax, specific bank has been mentioned for every Central Excise Commissionerate. If Service Tax amount is deposited in a branch of bank other than the nominated bank, it amounts to non-payment of Service Tax.

Precautions to be taken while depositing the Service Tax: while depositing the Service Tax the assessee should take the following precautions, at the time of paying the Service Tax:

- Service Tax should be paid within the time limit laid down in this regard.
- It should be deposited in the specified branches of the bank designated for this purpose in each Central Excise Commissionerate.
- The major head and sub-head relating to the service provided by the assessee should be correctly filled in the TR-6 challan.
- The TR-6 challan should be yellow in colour and should be filled in quintriplicate after being properly filled.

- In case of delay in making payment of Service Tax in time, the interest is also required to be paid at a simple rate of one and half percent for each month or part of the month for which payment is delayed.

If a person liable to pay tax is fails to do so within the prescribed period than shall pay simple interest at the rate not below 10 per cent and not exceeding 36 per cent per annum as for the time being fixed by the Central Government by notification in the Official Gazette. The Central Government has notified the rate of 13 percent per annum for the purpose of levy of interest from 10/09/2004.

It a person liable to pay Service Tax has fails to pay it shall pay in addition to interest and the penalty which shall not be less than two hundred rupees for every day during which such failures continues or at the rate of two per cent of such tax per month whichever is higher, starting with the first day after the due date till the date of actual payment. It should also be noted that total amount of penalty payable shall not exceed the Service Tax payable.

Facility for adjusting excess payment of Service Tax by the assessee towards future liability is also provided is law. In cases, where an assessee has paid to the credit of Central Government Service Tax in respect of a taxable service which is not provided by him for any reason, the assesseee can adjust the excess Service Tax paid by him calculated on a pro-rata basis against his Service Tax liability for the subsequent period, provided that the assessee has refunded the value of taxable service and Service Tax thereon to the person from whom it was received.

E-PAYMENT OF THE TAX

Service Tax Rules, 1994 states that the assesses shall deposit. The Service Tax I the designated bank in Form TR-6 within the time limit specified in Rule 6(1). The rule was effective from 1-10-2006 and make it compulsory for the assesses who has paid Service Tax of Rs. 50 Lakhs or above in the proceeding financial year or who has already paid Service Tax of Rs. 50 Lakhs in financial year shall deposit the Service tax liable to be paid by him electronically. It is compulsory from 1-10-2006.

For e-payment of the service, the taxpayer needs to have an account in any branch of the designated banks. For availing facility of e-payment, the Service Tax-payer will have to obtain user id and password from the bank in which he has the account. The procedure for e-payment is that the Service tax payer would log on to the website of the bank with his user i.d. and password. He will than choose the option of payment of Service Tax. On choosing this option the service taxpayer will be guided to e-payment portal wherein he would be filing the challan for payment of Service Tax and would authorized payment of Service tax by way of debit to his account. On submission, copy of acknowledgement and challans would be generated for the records of Service Tax payer.

The advantage of e-payment includes easy of operation, convenience, availability of payment 24 hours, online filing of challan and payment of taxes avoiding queues and waiting, instant cyber receipt for payment made, delivery of challan at doorsteps, free service or as the case may be at nominal cost etc. There by reducing the compliance cost.

EXEMPTIONS FORM THE LEVY OF SERVICE TAX

Central Government is empowered to grant exemption from the levy of Service Tax. Time to time Central Government has issued various notifications for exempting different taxable services. If the Central Government is satisfied that it is in the public interest than it may issue notification in the official Gazette to exempt that service. Certain services are exempted from the levy of Service Tax due to various reasons *e.g.* diplomatic exigencies, economic reasons and the overall public interest of the country. Some of them are initially exempted through the Finance Act, 1994 when Service Tax introduced service provided in Jammu & Kashmir were exempted because of the special constitutional status of the state. If a person from Jammu & Kashmir provides services outside Jammu & Kashmir in any other part of India, that service was made taxable, as location where service is provided is relevant. Merely because office is situated in Jammu & Kashmir does not mean that service is provided in Jammu & Kashmir.

Exemption was granted in the year 2002, to all services provided to United Nations or an International Organization. Exemption was also granted in the year 2007 to Diplomatic mission for official use of taxable services and also the officers and their families for personal use of taxable services. To encourage the earning of foreign exchange was crucial for India's economic development. Therefore, it was considered appropriate to exempt export of services. Therefore, services provided to all developers of Special Economic Zone (SEZ) or units of SEZ were exempted in the year 2004. Port services, Good transport services and containerized transport services received by an exporter and used for export of goods are also exempt through the notification of 2007.

In 2005, micro and small service providers are exempted from the levy of Service Tax. Small units whose turnover is less than Rs. 4 lakhs per annum are exempted, in 2007 this limit raised to Rs. 8 lakhs per annum and in 2008 it's further raised to Rs. 10 lakhs. All type of taxable services rendered by the Reserve Bank of India is exempted from the Service Tax. Value of goods and materials sold by the service provider to the recipient of service during the course of providing any taxable service, provided that no CENVAT Credit has been taken on such goods and materials, or, if CENVAT credit has been taken, such credit is paid before affecting the sale.

Certain exemptions are specific to each and every service. They are some times provided in the definition of services itself or through specific notifications. This system of providing exemption has became so complex that it's a tremendous task to find out that whether a service is taxable or exempted under the law.

ADMINISTRATIVE MACHINERY

The tax administration is an important aspect of tax management in a country. It is, therefore desirable that tax administration must receive adequate attention if the tax policy is to be fully attended. It is because in the absence of a diligent execution of taxes, inefficient enforcement of existing taxes and inequity among the taxpayer might defeat the very basic purpose of taxation. If the tax administration is good and taxing principles are adequate the income of the state increases. An efficient tax administration minimizes the cost of collection of tax. An increase in the government revenue is most important for economic development of the country. A neat and healthy tax administration is also essential to make the tax more equitable and revenue elastic.

Even the best and ideal tax policy measure supported by a just legal system if incapable of enforcement through efficient administrative machinery might prove futile in fulfillment of its objectives. It may lead not only to public irritation and ill feeling but even defeat its own purpose. In fact in the words of Colbert, the art of taxation consists in so plucking the goose as to obtain the largest amount of feathers with the least possible amount of hissing. This demands that the administering personnel should discharge their routine task with the maximum amount of endeavor and patience, consistent with efficiency.

Developing countries have a number of bottle-necks. In a developing economy people are uneducated and their income is also comparatively much lower leading to a low level of standard of living. Therefore, when taxes are levied on people in such economies they have comparatively greater temptation to evade taxes by different devices for every tax deprives the taxpayers of their purchasing power. Thus, in developing countries special attention needs to be given on the efficiency and simplicity of the administrative procedure so as to be understood by the general public to fulfill their obligations through voluntary compliance. In this regard the public awareness through advertisement in electronic media and newspapers is necessary.

In India the tax has been administered and levied by basically two departments namely Central Board of Excise and Customs and Central Board of Direct Taxes. The Central Board of Direct Taxes look after the direct taxes and Central Board of Excise and Customs (CBEC) looks indirect taxes including matter related to Service Tax and Central Sales Tax *etc*..The CBEC has a chairman assisted by members. The hierarchy for the jurisdiction of Service Tax is as follows:

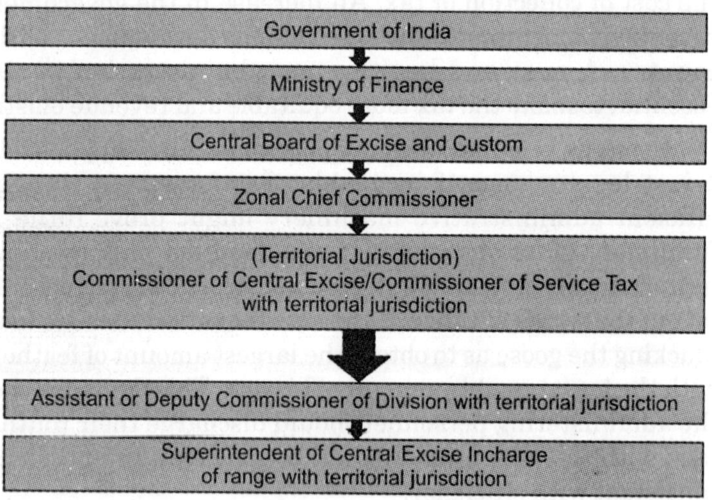

Fig. 4.2 : Jurisdiction of Service Tax

The CBEC has all India jurisdiction each chief commissioner has jurisdiction over a few Commissioners. The Commissioner has jurisdiction over few AC/DC who are also called Divisional officers. Each Division has five to six

Superintendent of Central Excise assisted by a handful of inspectors.

Administration of Service Tax

With the introduction of Service Tax, the Central Government had issued several instructions on administration of Service Tax. It was contemplated to create a cell/division in the headquarter office of the Commissionerate, headed by an Assistant Commissioner to deal with the matters relating to Service Tax. These instructions were issued with intention that for payment of Service Tax the assesses interact with senior officers of the Department so that suitable guidance was available to them and proper client friendly relationship is maintained. It was also expected that assesses paying Service Tax shall pay the same in centralized office instead of running from range to range or division to division. Service provider in most of the cases being a single individual would not have resources to ascertain and know the proper range officer to whom he is supposed to interact for purposes of Service Tax. Therefore, in the beginning there was a centralized Service Tax administration. But in the year 1998, the Board felt that centralized administration of Service Tax at the Commissionerate headquarter has great administrative inconvenience for the Department as well as the assesses. With the addition of more services, the problem is further complicated as the number of assesses requiring registration become too many. Therefore the Board felt that the Service Tax work need be decentralized from the Commissionerate Headquarters office to Divisional Headquarters. Such Divisional officers are to work with an officer of the rank of Superintendent of Central Excise to be incharge for the purposes of assessment and collection of Service Tax etc.

Director General of Service Tax

The post of Director General of Service Tax was created in the year 1997 to oversee smooth collection of Service Tax.

The functions of the Director General of Service Tax are as given below:

(*i*) The Director General is to ensure that proper establishment and infrastructure has been created under different Central Excise Commissionerate to monitor the collection and assessment of Service Tax;

(*ii*) He is to study the staff requirement for proper and effective implementation of Service Tax;

(*iii*) The Director General have to study as to how the various service taxes are being implemented in the field and to suggest measures as may be necessary to increase revenue collection or to streamline procedures;

(*iv*) The Director General is to undertake analysis of law and procedure in relation to Service Tax with a view to simplify the Service Tax collection and assessment;

(*v*) The Director General is also required to study and create a data bank on collection of Service Tax from the date of its inception and to monitor the revenue collection from Service Tax. He should also get the same data updated from time to time;

(*vi*) The Director General shall also inspect the Service Tax Cells in the Commissionerate to ensure that they are functioning effectively;

(*vii*) The Director General is also required to associate himself as an extended arm of the Board for conducting study as may be assigned.

Setting up of Service Tax Commissionerate

Due to the growing importance of Service Tax, Commissionerate in six cities viz. Delhi, Mumbai, Kolkata, Chennai, Bangalore and Ahmadabad are established. These Service Tax Commissionerate will have full fledged operations like Central Excise Commissionerate. The role of such Commissionerate would be to indentify new services which could be taxed and to ensure compliance Service Tax payments. The following table gives the jurisdiction of the Commissionerate:

Table 4.3: Jurisdiction of the Commissionerate of Service Tax

Sl. No.	Designation	Jurisdiction
1.	Commissioner of Service Tax, Mumbai	Central Excise Zone of Mumbai-I & II except Raged Commissionerate
2.	Commissioner of Service Tax, Delhi	Central Excise Zone of Delhi except Commissionerate of Panchkula & Rohtak.
3.	Commissioner of Service Tax, Chennai	Central Excise Zone of Chennai-I & Chennai-II
4.	Commissioner of Service Tax, Kolkata	Central Excise zone of Kolkata except Cimmissionerate of Bolpur, Siliguri & Haldia
5.	Commisioner of Service Tax, Bangalore	Central Excise Zone of Bangalore.
6.	Commissioner of Service Tax, Ahmedabad	Central Excise Zone of Ahmedabad I & II

The work load of Service Tax administration is continuously increasing therefore it requires separate comprehensive legislation along with distinct administrative machinery exclusively devoted to imposition and collection of Service Tax. This would bring greater clarity among the taxpayers and the main objective behind the levy of Service Tax *i.e.* revenue maximization could be achieved and the scope for tax evasion and avoidance be minimized.

REVENUE COLLECTION FROM SERVICE TAX

The revenue collection from Service Tax is very encouraging

and shows that this becomes a major contributor of revenue. This can be evident from the following table and chart:

Table 4.4: Service Tax Revenue and Percentage Growth

Financial Year	Revenue (Rs. Crores)	Per cent Growth	Number of Assessees	Per cent Growth over previous year
1994-95	410	Base year	3943	Base year
1995-96	846	106.34	4866	19
1996-97	1022	20.80	13982	187
1997-98	1515	48.23	45991	228
1998-99	1787	17.95	107479	133
1999-2000	2072	15.94	115495	7
2000-01	2540	22.58	122326	6
2001-02	3305	30.11	187577	53
2002-03	4125	24.81	232048	24
2003-04	7890	91.27	403856	74
2004-05	14196	79.58	740267	92
2005-06	23053	62.39	806585	9.18
2006-07	38169	65.57	918746	-
2007-08	50603	32.57	NA	-
2008-09(R.E.)	65000	28.45	NA	-
2009-10(B.E.)	68900	06.00	NA	-

Source: Compiled from Service Tax Annual Performance Report 2005-06, Economic Survey, Budget Document various issues.

The revenue receipts from the Service Tax shows steady rise since its imposition. The tax collection in the year 1994-95 was Rs. 410 crores increased to Rs. 846 crores in 1995-96 and shows a tremendous growth of 106.34 percent. In 1996-97 it increased to Rs. 1022 crores, in 1997-98 to Rs. 1515 crores, in 1998-99 to Rs.1787 crores, in 1999-2000 to

Rs. 2072 crores, in 2000-01 to Rs. 2540 crores, in 2001-02 to Rs. 3305 crores, in 2002-03 to Rs. 425 crores, in 2003-04 to Rs. 7890 crores, on 2004-05 to Rs. 14196 crores, in 2005-06 to Rs. 23053 crores, in 2006-07 to Rs. 38169 crores, in 2007-08 to Rs. 50603 crores, in 2008-09 to Rs. 65000 crores and expected to increase to Rs. 68900 crores in the year 2009-10. The trend shows continuous increase in the revenue.

There has been a considerable increase in the number of assessee. We can say that the assessee base has grown even more sharply that is from 3943 assessee in 1994-95, the number of assessee have grown by 19 per cent in the next year and the number increased to 4866 assessee. The numbers of assessee shows continuous growth and reached the figure of 918746 in the year 2006-07.

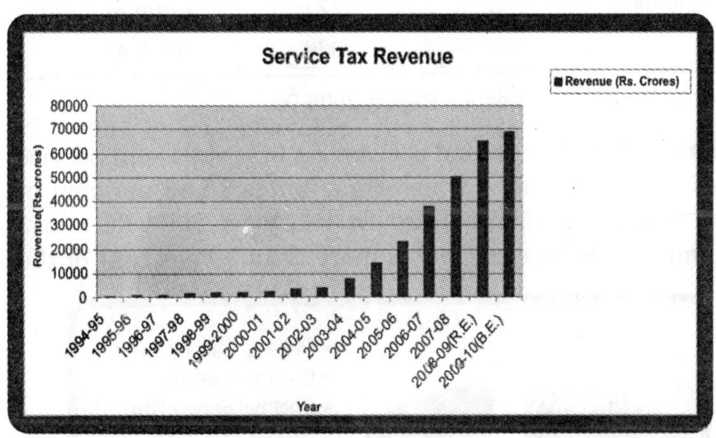

Fig. 4.3

Source: Compiled from Service Tax Annual Performance Report 2005-06, Economic Survey, Budget Document various issues.

The table 4.5 depicts the revenue collection from the top ten Commissionerate for the year 2005-06. Total contribution of these Commissionerate is 72.82 per cent of the overall receipts of Service Tax which clearly indicates that service sector is presently concentrated in bigger cities. Out of these, Mumbai alone contributes 30.79 per cent of the total receipts

Table 4.5: Top Ten Commissionerates: 2005-06

Commissionerate	2004-05	2005-06
Mumabai Service Tax	3980	7099.05
Delhi Service Tax	1999	3559.15
Chennai Service Tax	1039	1566.48
Bangalore Service Tax	761	1259.22
Kolkata Service Tax	807	1094.01
Pune-III	337	629.62
Hyderabad-II	333	568.37
Ahmadabad Service Tax	241	383.55
Rajkot	248	320.59
Chandigarh	221	308.37
Total	9966	16788.41

Source: Annual Performance Report 2005-06

of Service Tax. The second position occupies by Delhi Service Tax Commissionerate which contributes 15.43 per cent of total Service Tax receipts. In the year 2004-05 these Commissionerate contributes more than 70 per cent of the

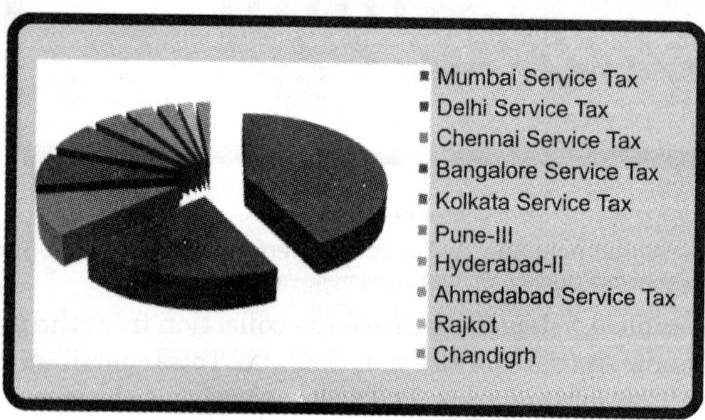

Fig. 4.4 : Top Ten Commissionerates: 2005-06

Source: Annual Performance Report 2005-06

total Service Tax revenue. Beside these the major revenue earning Commissionerate are Chennai- Service Tax, Bangalore Service Tax, Kolkata Service Tax, Pune-III, Hyderabad-II, Ahmadabad Service Tax, Rajkot, Chandigarh. This indicates that presently Service Tax revenue receipts are concentrated in bigger cities but there is an ample scope and potential for larger Service Tax collection at other location also.

Table 4.6: Service-wise Revenue for 2005-06 vis-à-vis 2004-05

Service	2005-06 Revenue	2004-05 Revenue	Actual increase/ decrease	% increase/ decrease
1	2	3	4	5
Stock Broker	823.57	375.89	447.68	119.01
Telephone	4092.49	3934.36	158.13	4.02
General Insurance	1253.98	1260.52	-6.54	-0.52
Advertising Services	436.62	351.08	84.82	24.11
Paging services	7.47	3.41	4.06	119.06
Courier Services	376.49	391.53	-15.04	-3.84
Customs House Agent	125.45	97.32	28.13	28.09
Steamer Agent	76.04	34.17	42.23	123.59
Mandap Keeper	146.07	112.03	34.67	30.95
Air Travl Agent	189.72	157.82	31.09	20.21
Manpower Recruitment or Supply Agency	312.68	64.36	248.32	385.83
Consulting Engineer	724.89	469.72	255.17	54.32
Clearing & Forwarding Agent	209.08	178.12	31.68	17.79
Rent-a-Cab Scheme operator	68.39	53.06	15.33	28.89
Outdoor Caterer	46.48	14.06	31.88	218.36
Pandal or Shamiana Contractor	36.45	19.26	17.19	89.25

(Contd...)

1	2	3	4	5
Tour Operator	95.37	4321.00	52.16	120.71
Goods Tranport Agency	1396.37	174.01	1396.37	702.05
Architect	99.53	74.11	25.42	34.03
Credit Rating Agency	13.03	11.63	1.04	12.04
Chartered Accountant	204.23	187.91	16.32	8.69
Cost Accountant	4.47	1.93	2.54	131.61
Interior Decorator	33.96	11.31	22.65	200.27
Market Research Agency	51.06	31.36	20.24	64.54
Company Secretary	31.21	8.02	23.19	289.15
Real Estate Agent	113.19	85.08	28.11	33.04
Security Agency	308.01	200.06	108.04	54.00
Underwriter	3.38	1.08	2.03	212.96
Management Consultant	392.59	208.13	184.46	88.63
Scientific or Technical Consultancy	102.58	73.35	29.23	39.85
Photography	58.37	70.97	-12.06	-17.75
Convention Service	40.56	16.98	23.58	138.87
Online Information & Database access or retrival	143.12	98.73	44.39	44.96
Broadcasting Agency or Organisation	415.27	272.95	142.32	52.14
Insurance Auxiliary Service	1216.17	713.29	502.88	70.05
Banking & other Financial Services	1953.76	1046.78	906.98	86.64
Port Service	654.03	610.68	43.62	7.14
Authorised Service Station	156.39	147.81	8.58	5.08
Video Tape Production	39.77	21.22	18.55	87.42
Sound Recording	10.71	9.25	1.46	15.78
Telegraph	67.93	97.11	-29.18	-30.05

(Contd...)

1	2	3	4	5
Telex	10.01	3.76	6.25	166.22
Facsimile	3.25	1.68	1.57	93.45
Leased Circuit	149.92	135.06	14.86	11.00
Life Insurance	361.29	295.68	65.61	22.19
Cargo Handling	167.94	95.13	72.81	76.54
Store & Warehousing	145.07	92.62	52.45	56.63
Event Management	56.05	33.74	22.76	67.46
Rail Travel Agent	6.02	4.17	2.03	48.68
Health Club & Fitness Centre	39.51	20.44	19.07	93.03
Beauty Parlour	26.81	17.88	8.93	49.94
Fasion Designing	6.44	8.13	-1.69	-20.79
Cable Operator	74.11	75.21	-1.01	-1.46
Dry Cleaning	13.13	11.07	2.06	18.61
Business Auxiliary Service	1470.44	527.22	943.22	178.09
Commercial Training or Coaching	195.36	109.75	85.61	78.00
Commissioning & Installation	441.55	137.05	304.05	221.13
Franchise Service	47.91	18.96	28.95	152.69
Internet Café	22.69	14.92	7.77	52.08
Maintenance or Repair Service	862.61	342.43	520.18	151.91
Technical Testing & Analysis	187.72	105.96	81.76	77.16
Business Auxiliary Service	54.01	10.18	43.92	431.43
Airport Services	332.07	58.56	273.51	467.06
Transport of Goods by Air	67.13	32.08	35.05	109.26

(Contd...)

1	2	3	4	5
Survey and Exploration of Minerals	83.07	6.47	76.06	1183.93
Opinion Poll Services	0.79	0.04	0.39	97.05
Intellectual Property Service	180.91	12.71	168.02	1323.37
Forward Contract	20.16	5.13	15.03	292.98
Television & Radio Programme Production	62.03	4.74	57.29	1208.65
Commercial or Industrial Construction Service	663.24	85.96	577.28	671.57
Travel Agents	6.14	2.82	3.32	117.73
Cleaning Service	29.68			
Construction of Residential Complex	85.55			
Dreadging Service	26.00			
Mailing List Compilation & Mailing	2.37			
Club or Association	19.65			
Packing Service	3.59			
Survey and Map Making	2.62			
Transport of goods through pipeline	120.29			
Site Preparation	20.42			
Misc	0.00			
Cess	451.13			
TOTAL	23052.94	14196.19		

Source: Annual Performance Report 2005-06

Service-wise Revenue for 2005-06 *vis-à-vis* 2004-05 of Select Services

The Table-4.6 compares the growth of revenue of services during 2005-06 over the year 2004-05. It shows that revenue from Stock Broker's services grew 119.10 per cent as compared to previous year. The other important service that shows a jump in revenue collections is Manpower Recruitment or Supply Agency. The revenue collection was Rs. 64.36 crores in 2004-05 which has gone up to Rs. 312.68 crores in 2005-06 *i.e.*385 per cent growth over the last year. Clearing and Forwarding Agent also indicates a rose of Rs. 31.68 crores over the last year. Goods Transport Agency (GTA) was reintroduced in the year 2004 have great potentiality. The revenue collection from GTA shows 702.05 per cent growth in 2005-06 over the year 2004-05. Business Auxiliary Service has grown from Rs. 527.22 crores to Rs. 1470.44 crores and increase of over 178 per cent. Courier, General Insurance, Photography, Telegraph, Fashion Designing, Cable Operator, are some of the services that shows negative growth over the last year which needs to be investigated.

First three services introduced in tax net in 1994 *i.e.* Telecom, General Insurance and Stockbrokers have conventionally contributed a lion's share in the overall revenue receipts. However, their dominance has been constantly on the decline as total receipts from these three services have fallen from 83 per cent in 1999-2000 to 40 per cent in 2004-05 and now 27 per cent in 2005-06. Whereas Telecom services remained supreme, the insurance services are No.2 and Stockbrokers services have gone down to No.9 position.

The Table-4.7 indicates the Zone-wise Service Tax collection for the year 2005-06. For the convenience of the collection of tax revenue Service Tax collection has been divided into 23 Zone *viz.* Ahmadabad, Bangalore, Bhopal, Bhubaneswar, Chandigarh, Chennai, Kerala, Coimbatore, Delhi, Shillong, Hyderabad, Jaipur, Kolkata, Lucknow, Mysore, Meerut, Mumbai-I, Mumbai-II, Nagpur, Pune, Ranchi, Vadodara, Vishakhapatnam. The revenue collection from Mumbai-I zone is highest among all zones which have collected Rs.7099.05 crores and the collection were 30.79 per cent of the total Service Tax receipts. The least revenue collection is from Shilong zone which is Rs. 128.20 crores and accounted 0.55 per cent of total Service Tax revenue.

Table 4.7: Zone-wise Service Tax Collection for F.Y. 2005-06

Name of the Zone	Revenue 2004-05	Number of Assessees	Revenue 2005-06	Number of Assessees
Ahemedabad	601.98	47130	859.99	5116
Bangalore	761.04	31422	1259.22	40141
Bhopal	274.57	43936	463.81	46339
Bhubneshwar	153.07	9782	263.94	11847
Chandigarh	386.15	33669	512.47	35908
Chennai	1092.72	38559	1645.36	41985
Kerala	355.78	33028	458.36	19274
Coimbatore	348.42	45962	460.96	45407
Delhi	2110.09	71319	3691.93	89384
Shillong	85.01	8587	128.02	9266
Hyderabad	437.75	20324	723.06	23692
Jaipur	280.19	45602	426.38	42540
Kolkata	941.45	32138	1270.04	37588
Lucknow	304.19	32548	464.33	36112
Mysore	191.14	20190	267.77	18970
Meerut	253.49	27692	459.81	28920
Mumbai-i	3979.68	89260	7099.05	110665
Mumbai-ii	130.76	2244	166.03	2542
Nagpur	231.35	33951	381.67	36661
Pune	514.44	40110	917.11	47295
Ranchi	164.18	14613	232.16	14785
Vadodara	216.63	30353	433.03	30952
Vishakhapatnam	211.76	22569	311.36	24766
Grand Total	14026.65	774988	22896.67	846155

Source: Annual Performance Report 2005-06

CHALLENGES BEFORE THE ADMINISTRATION OF SERVICE TAX

Administration of Service Tax in India has multi-dimensional challenges. Some of them are related to nature and growth of service sector in our economy and others relate to the procedural aspect of the Service Tax collection. The growth of service sector at high speed offers opportunity as well as challenges to bring under the tax net hitherto uncovered services. This offers tremendous revenue potential to the government. A planned liberalized and globalized process requires levying the tax on new services without substantial rise in the rate or cost of collection. This approach requires a suitable classification of the services through grouping them on the basis of their nature and characteristics. It will help in reorganizing various services and would provide clear cut guidelines for administrator and taxpayer (service provider) to understand their liability properly. Too many exemptions and exceptions provide an opportunity for taking of certain services out of the tax net. As a matter of fact definitional confusion does help in proliferating litigation which is an unnecessary waste of money, time and energy. RBI has classified the services into three categories viz. Producer's Services, Consumer's Services and Government Services. WTO classification is more suitable in globalized economy and would facilitate international trade. In this regard WTO classification of services into twelve broad categories could be beneficially adopted.

INCIDENCE OF TAX

Measuring the effect of a particular tax provision is an arduous. However, such a study is of utmost importance for the policy makers in determining the tax base, rates and selecting the persons who could be the realer burden of the tax. It may help in understanding the buoyancy of a particular tax measures and help in providing the basis for any change in the tax structure. It might substantially affect the demand and supply of a particular product or service. It is practically not possible to measure with accuracy the effect of a tax on the various player of the economic development. The difficulty arises because of the reason that the demand and supply and buoyancy of a particular tax are affect due to numerable socio-economic factors. Taxation is merely one of the factors and sometimes a meager factor to influence the economic effects.

In the area of indirect taxes because of the features of tax-shifting the burden of tax does not fall on the person who collect and deposit the same in the treasury he do not bear the real burden of the tax. He merely acts as the agent of the revenue department. The real burden falls ultimately on the consumers. In the economic sense it is termed as 'economic incidence' (in short 'incidence') of a tax. A study of economic consequence of Service Tax in general and particularly in respect of each services and the factors that influence the behavior of the consumer and helping the policy makers to modify the list of taxable services accordingly.

The terms 'tax incidence', 'tax burden', 'impact' and 'effect' are used 'rather loosely in the available economic literature and in the popular press'. Incidence of Service Tax is concerned with the person who bear real burden on whom the real money burden falls i.e. the consumer of services. Impact is to be seen in the context of the consumer as well as the service provider. Effect is a comprehensive term which is concerned with the overall effect of Service Tax on the economic development, treasury and the social- economical life structure of the community.

BUOYANCY OF SERVICE TAX

The buoyancy of a particular tax with respect to national income is the ratio of the relative change in the tax revenue to relative change in national income. It is another way of examining tax revenue performance which is a measure of responsiveness of tax revenue to the change in the national income.

While considering the improvement in the tax revenue it is total change in revenue which covers the changes due to rates, coverage and administrative change also. Buoyancy estimate helps to examine improvement in tax revenue which arises due to an expansion in the base. Since the taxes are levied on the economic activities, the national income can be used as proxy to the tax base. Thus, the percentage change in the tax revenue due to one-percent change in national income is known as buoyancy. If one per cent increase in the national income leads to more than one per cent change in tax revenue than the tax revenue is said to be buoyant. The more buoyant the tax revenue is better for the government.

Buoyancy can be calculated by taking the ratio of percentage change in national income. This is a crude method of calculating buoyancy because in this method we take the value of the variable in the initial year and in the final year into consideration. Statistically, buoyancy can be estimated by filling a log-linear regression of tax revenue on national income. It is a more satisfactory method because it takes into account each value of two variables over the period of time.

Buoyancy co-efficient can be calculated by adopting the statistical technique of regression analysis which is as follows:

$Y = \alpha_0 X^{\alpha 1} U_i$

Or,

$\text{Log } y_i = \log \alpha_0 + \alpha_1 \log x_i + \log u_i$

Where,

Y is tax revenue;

X is national income;

α_0 is level of tax yield when independent variable has a zero value;

α_1 is buoyancy;

$\log y_i$ is service tax in log form;

$\log x_i$ is NNP at factor cost in log form; and

u_i if standard error.

There will be three cases in tax buoyancy:

Case I

If $\alpha_1 > 1$

It shows that due to Re. 1 enhancement in NNP, will result in more than Re. 1 Enhancement in Service Tax.

Case II

If $\alpha_1 = 1$

It shows that due to Re. 1 enhancement in NNP will result Re. 1 enhancement in Service Tax also.

Case III

If $\alpha_1 < 1$

It shows that due to Re. 1 enhancement in NNP will result in less than Re. 1 enhancement in Service Tax.

In order to estimate the buoyancy of Service Tax the data in the table 4.8 has been used.

Table 4.8: NNP and Service Tax Revenue

Financial Year	NNP at FC (Rs. Crores) (X)	Service Tax (Rs. Crores) (Y)
1	2	3
1994-95	818334	410
1995-96	958679	846
1996-97	1119238	1022
1997-98	1244980	1515
1998-99	1438913	1787
1999-00	1589672	2072
2000-01	1700467	2540

1	2	3
2001-02	1849360	3305
2002-03	1994248	4125
2003-04	2239939	7890
2004-05	2526408	14196
2005-06	2870750	23053
2006-07	3325817	38169
2007-08	3787597	50603
2008-09	4394913	65000

Source: Compiled from Service Tax Annual Performance Report 2005-06, Economic Survey, Budget Document various issues.

Table 4.9: Buoyancy of Service Tax (1994-2009) Regression Results

Constant	Coefficient	R^2	D-W Statistic
36.8247 (18.98)	3.1358 (23.38)	0.9768	0.5456

*Figures in the brackets are t-values

The buoyancy of Service Tax has been calculated through regression method and the buoyancy coefficient is 3.1358 which indicates that if there is Re 1 enhancement in national income or NNP there will be more than three-fold increase in Service Tax revenue i.e. 3.1358 times increment in Service Tax revenue. This indicates that the tax is very much buoyant. This shows that the revenue collection from the tax is very much and in future it will be the one of the most potential tax. By comparing the buoyancy of Service Tax with other taxes we can find that the buoyancy coefficients of different taxes are much lower than the Service Tax. The buoyancy coefficient from income tax is 1.47, corporation tax is 1.18, and excise duty is 0.72, customs duty 1.02.[9] The buoyancy coefficient of Excise Duty is lowest among the all which indicates that revenue performance of the particular tax is less than the national income and also depicts that the role of manufacturing sector is declining and the buoyancy coefficient of Service Tax indicates the performance level of service sector is increasing as compare to manufacturing sector.

FUTURE PROSPECTS OF THE TAX

While recognizing the potential of service tax there are few points worth mentioning. A large number of uncovered services were in the nature of intermediate services like various professional services and bringing them into tax net without providing for abatement of input duty credit will create distortions in the tax structure. There are also definitional difficulties in valuation of real estate and construction services which are in the nature of durable goods and sometimes self-supplied. Finally, a large number of small units scattered all over the country raising the administrative costs of collecting these taxes. Therefore, while service tax is a promising area, covering more services would require abandoning the selective approach of covering certain services and going for an integrated approach. This would require a single GST legislation with full input tax credit. Such a move will boost the tax to GDP ratio and widen the tax base, providing the much-needed financial succor to public finance in India.

FEASIBILITY OF GST IN INDIA

Goods and Service Tax (GST) system is considered as the most successful stage of indirect tax reform throughout the world. Tax Reform Committee 1991 in its report envisaged that:

> We must ensure that there will be a unified and rational system of taxation of services applicable to the whole country. This means that the service tax must be part of value added tax in course of time and should be levied at

> the Central level. A cascading type of services tax should be avoided at all costs. We envisage that as the Union excise on commodities get gradually transformed into a value added tax at manufacturing level, the service tax will get woven into that system and therefore tax could be levied also on services that enter into the productive processes.

Further,

> The Modvat system should be gradually converted into a comprehensive value added tax at manufacturing stage. Once this is done it would be possible to introduce a fairly comprehensive system of taxation of services also on the basis of value added principle so that the entire system of indirect taxation at the Central level would be devoid of cascading and would cause no distortion in cost or in the allocation of resources.

During the last five years, the Ministry of Finance is tinkering with the task of formulating the policy, modality and the form of shifting to a comprehensive system of indirect tax. The Finance Minister observed that in para. 119 of the budget speech of 2004-05:

> It is my intention to align India's tariff structure to those of ASEAN countries. Eventually, there should be a uniform rate of tax on goods and services.

The same view was reiterated in the Budget Speech of 2005-06 in the para. 94:

> In the medium to long term, it is my goals that the entire production-distribution chain should be covered by a National VAT or even better a goods and service tax, encompassing both the Centre and State.

The budget Speech of 2006-07 in para. 155 made a positive remark about GST:

> It is my sense that there is large consensus that the country should move towards a national level Goods and Service Tax (GST) that should be shared between the Centre and the State. I propose that we set April 1, 2010 as the date

> for introduction of GST. World over goods and services attract the same rate of tax. That is the foundation of the GST. People must get used to the idea of GST. Hence we must progressively converge the service tax rate and the CENVAT rate.....

The budget speech of 2007-08 made a more emphatic move towards GST. In para 116:

> I wish to record my deep appreciation of the spirit of co-operative federalism displayed by State Governments and especially their Finance Ministers. At my request, the Empowered Committee of State Finance Ministers has agreed to work with the Central Government to prepare a roadmap for introducing a national level Goods and Services Tax (GST) with effect from April 1, 2010.

In the budget speech of 2008-09 in the para 183 Finance Minister says:

> Following an agreement between the Central Government and the State Government the rate of Central Sales Tax was reduced from four per cent to three per cent in this financial year. It is now proposed to reduce the rate to two per cent from April 1, 2008. Consultations are underway on the compensation for the losses, if any, and once agreement is reached the new rate will be notified. I am also happy to report that there is considerable progress in repairing a road map for introducing the Goods and Service Tax with effect from April 1, 2010.

In the recent budget of 2009-10 Finance Minister made it clear that India is going to implement GST from April 1, 2010. He observed that the Empowered Committee of the State Finance Ministers has made considerable progress in preparing the design of the GST and have reached an agreement on the basic structure in keeping with the principle of Fiscal Federalism enshrined in the Constitution. He declared that:

> The broad contour of the GST model is that it will be a dual GST comprising of a Central GST and a State GST.

> The Centre and State will each legislate, levy and administer the Central GST and State GST, respectively.

He promised that the Central Government shall continue to play catalytic role to facilitate the introduction of GST by April 1, 2010.

The task is challenging. To meet the deadline for the implementation of GST is not impossible though formidable. The first and foremost issue is that the government has yet to decide the fact as to how the States would be empowered to levy Service Tax. Presently, under the framework of fiscal federalism enshrined in the Constitution the States have no power to impose Service Tax. The taxing power of Centre and State in the Indian federal polity is well defined. States have already 19 taxing entries in its kitty in contrast with the only 14 entries in the Union List. Enhancing taxing power of the States through giving them right to tax on services is fraught with several conflicts. The past experience of creating the chaotic situation on the exercise of the power to impose tax on sale of goods should be kept in mind, so that history may not be repeated. It will further complicate the system rather than simplifying it.

The Empowered Committee of the State Finance Ministers is preparing the roadmap for the introduction of GST. In spite of strong determination and political consensus for adopting GST the actual shape to come is still uncertain. The model of GST as being enforced in several countries should only be considered as only guidelines. Any attempt to adopt a particular model of GST is not suitable in the context of the Indian quasi federal constitution which has unique features. It has several unitary features which empower the Centre to control the States. The distribution of taxing power in Centre and States indicates this fact very clearly especially entry 97. This entry vested the residuary power in the Union Government. The power to impose tax on services though earlier validated under entry 97, presently after the 88th Amendment of the Constitution of India is clearly provided in entry 92C. Under the aforesaid circumstances if dual GST is to be implemented throughout India, the States are to be empowered by a constitutional amendment to levy and collect tax on services as well.

Presently the States could only be allowed to collect GST on intra- state services only. The States may collect and appropriate the whole revenue. The Union should continue to collect Service Tax as at present excluding the intra-state services. This arrangement may not require any further constitutional amendment. As far as the rate structure is concerned there should be a uniform rate of GST. The resulting loss if any would be met to a great extent by the additional revenue rose through tax on services as well. If there is some loss of revenue occur to States it would be compensated by the Union Government. The Union Government should continue to impose GST on all India services and inter-state transactions of goods and services. The only problem here would be with the proposed abolition of CST rates of which has been slashed from four per cent to two per cent and is naturally being phased out. But the rate of GST would be just the double for such transactions of goods. So this situation requires some favourable consideration of inter-state transactions of goods and services. However, the availability of credit for taxes already paid at earlier stages of the transition of goods and services would compensate the comparatively higher burden of taxes on inter-state transitions. Thus, the transaction to GST is expected to be smooth and revenue neutral in respect of its impact on the taxpayers.

In India the existing constitutional framework, the political environment, economic slow down and several other circumstances raise fundamental doubts in meeting the deadline *i.e.* 1st April 2010 for a shift to GST. The one suitable alternative which is feasible is to start with Central GST with full credit of past taxes. The state VAT should be retained in respect of goods only on intra-state transaction. If the aforesaid suggestion is implemented then it may not presently require any constitutional amendment and the dateline fixed could be attained.

REFERENCES

1. Fisher Irving; *The Nature and Concept of Income*: 52 (New York, 1906) here it is not felt necessary to enter into the controversy of Haig-Simon and Irving Fisher's opinion on the concept of income.
2. *Ibid.* at 106.
3. *The Hindu*, Saturday 1st August 2009, p.14
4. Budget Speech 1994-95, Para 87, Part B
5. Report of the Tax Reform Committee (1991) constituted under the chairmanship of Dr. Raja J. Chelliah, at 122-123.
6. Budget Speech, 2000-01, Para-126, Part B.
7. Education Cess on the amount of Service Tax.
8. Addition Higher Education Cess on the amount.
9. The buoyancy coefficient of different taxes have been sourced from Report on Currency and Finance, Reserve Bank of India, Mumbai, 2005, at IV-10

5

Revenue Contribution of Some Special Services

The availability of information regarding revenue realized by the government individual services are of utmost importance for determining the efficiency and efficacy of imposition of Service Tax. However the availability of the reliable data in this respect should be easily made available and accessible. The Annual Performance Report of Director General of Service Tax is available only for the year 2005-06. In the absence of current information in this regard the present chapter is confined and based on this report. Out of 83 taxable services till 2005-06 we have selected 30 specific services as a sample of analysis in this chapter. These groups of sample services are analyzed and divided into three categories on the basis of the revenue collection for the year 2005-06. For detail see Table-5.1. On the basis of above data we have divided the services into three categories. These categories are as follows:

- Top ten revenue contributor services;
- Bottom ten revenue contributor services; and
- Some services with wider scope.

Table 5.1 : Service-wise Revenue Trend from 1994-95 to 2005-06

(Rs. in crores)

Services	1994-95	1995-96	1996-97	1997-98	1998-99	1999-2000	2000-01	2001-02	2002-03	2003-04	2004-05	2005-06
Stock Broker*	35.45	44.38	50.75	55.95	66.48	185.62	282.24	280.76	101.23	249.99	375.89	823.57
Telephone#	202.05	493.40	580.94	716.38	834.65	1176.79	1087.17	1382.84	1578.21	2692.33	3934.36	4092.49
General* Insurance	173.11	308.38	355.04	379.15	405.08	351.31	472.95	553.70	644.49	1039.58	1260.52	1253.98
Advertising$			19.33	89.75	89.73	86.18	110.47	150.18	174.73	220.29	351.80	436.62
Pager#			5.36	9.20	12.63	21.01	68.78	41.47	6.26	3.13	3.41	7.47
Courier$			10.59	48.30	45.84	63.43	110.39	111.62	127.23	227.01	391.53	376.49
C.H.As				15.79	24.22	18.06	23.09	30.91	32.66	80.34	97.32	125.45
Steamer Agent				11.43	17.73	11.90	13.91	12.11	12.38	32.12	34.17	76.4
Mandap Keeper				14.73	23.45	20.55	41.82	48.07	35.09	53.22	112.03	146.7
Air Travel Agent				22.82	37.15	24.51	42.92	46.36	51.46	87.00	157.82	189.72
Manpower Recruitment Agency				3.82	8.32	7.00	12.69	12.81	20.50	30.67	64.36	312.68
Consulting Engineer*				37.93	84.01	43.97	97.18	94.47	148.15	280.68	469.72	724.89
C & F Agent$				19.13	37.26	18.88	52.24	52.24	59.13	118.41	178.12	209.80
Rent-a-Cab				1.37	2.39	0.32	7.14	10.96	15.43	28.50	53.06	68.39

(Contd...)

Services	1994-95	1995-96	1996-97	1997-98	1998-99	1999-2000	2000-01	2001-02	2002-03	2003-04	2004-05	2005-06
Outdoor Caterer				3.96	1.52	0.26	0.00	0.23	0.23	0.00	14.60	46.48
Pandal/Shamiana				3.97	1.46	0.28	0.00	0.14	0.54	0.00	19.26	36.45
Tour Operator				8.37	4.06	0.22	8.24	11.28	12.50	30.95	43.21	95.37
G.T.O./G.T.A*				73.85	72.45	-14.52	24.58	6.75	5.13	0.00	174.10	1396.37
Architect					1.38	4.59	15.15	17.61	22.09	36.42	74.11	99.53
Credit Rating Agency@					0.57	1.79	2.56	3.69	11.26	13.14	11.63	13.03
Chartered Accountant$					2.80	10.75	37.13	62.57	74.60	114.04	187.91	204.23
Cost Accountant@					0.06	0.27	0.35	0.35	1.22	1.08	1.93	4.47
Interior Decorator					0.26	1.06	1.87	0.01	4.93	6.15	11.31	33.96
Market Research Agency					2.12	3.85	9.49	10.61	14.52	20.83	31.36	51.60
Company Secretary					0.02	0.43	0.16	0.47	3.13	0.10	8.02	31.21
Real Estate Agent					0.93	2.50	7.79	9.22	11.37	28.99	85.08	113.19
Security Agency					5.36	13.93	37.38	40.88	62.11	118.02	200.06	308.10
Underwriter@					0.01	0.33	1.79	2.21	2.50	2.17	1.08	3.38
Management Consultant					4.30	16.56	42.20	48.71	65.48	122.99	208.13	392.59

(Contd...)

Services	1994-95	1995-96	1996-97	1997-98	1998-99	1999-2000	2000-01	2001-02	2002-03	2003-04	2004-05	2005-06
Scientific or Technical Consultancy								3.66	15.12	28.70	73.35	102.58
Photography								11.11	31.78	48.22	70.97	58.37
Convention Service								1.53	4.68	8.19	16.98	40.56
Online Information & Database access or retrival								12.84	40.53	68.12	98.73	143.12
Broadcasting Agency or Organisation$								13.25	90.45	177.48	272.95	415.27
Insurance Auxiliary Service*								34.24	104.83	273.43	713.29	1216.17
Banking & other financial services*								44.70	174.56	307.65	1046.78	1953.76
Port Service$								90.26	194.47	359.45	610.68	654.30
Authorized Service Station								16.69	50.58	78.98	147.81	156.39
Video Tape Production								2.77	8.10	10.88	21.22	39.77
Sound Recording								0.71	5.92	12.40	9.25	10.71

(Contd...)

Services	1994-95	1995-96	1996-97	1997-98	1998-99	1999-2000	2000-01	2001-02	2002-03	2003-04	2004-05	2005-06
Telegraph#								9.10	4.53	23.31	97.11	67.93
Telex#								0.50	2.85	5.37	3.76	10.01
Facsimile#								0.63	0.69	0.65	1.68	3.25
Leased Circuit#								17.88	36.67	77.21	135.06	149.92
Life Insurance									23.50	320.04	295.68	361.29
Cargo Handling									10.45	30.04	95.13	167.94
Store & Warehousing									9.71	63.03	92.62	145.07
Event Management									2.28	17.47	33.74	56.50
Rail Travel Agent@									0.69	2.03	4.17	6.20
Health Club & Fitness Centre									2.22	10.88	20.44	39.51
Beauty Parlour									2.61	7.71	17.88	26.81
Fashion Designing@									0.48	1.46	8.13	6.44
Cable Operator									7.64	44.78	75.21	74.11
Dry Cleaning									0.94	4.12	11.07	13.13
Business Auxiliary Service*										49.80	527.22	1470.44

(Contd...)

Services	1994-95	1995-96	1996-97	1997-98	1998-99	1999-2000	2000-01	2001-02	2002-03	2003-04	2004-05	2005-06
Commercial training or Coaching$										29.68	109.75	195.36
Commissionig & Installation$										23.80	137.50	441.55
Franchise Service										5.49	18.96	47.91
Internet Café										3.94	14.92	22.69
Maintenance or Repair Service*										90.59	342.43	862.61
Technical Testing & Analysis										58.74	105.96	187.72
Business Exhibition											10.18	54.10
Airport Services$											58.56	332.07
Transport of Goods by Air											32.08	67.13
Survey and Exploration of Minerals											6.47	83.07
Opinion Poll Services@											0.47	0.79
Intellectual Property Service											12.71	180.91

(Contd...)

Services	1994-95	1995-96	1996-97	1997-98	1998-99	1999-2000	2000-01	2001-02	2002-03	2003-04	2004-05	2005-06
Forward Contract											5.13	20.16
Television & Radio Programme Production											4.74	62.03
Commercial or Industrial Construction Service*											85.96	663.24
Travel Agents@											2.82	6.14
Cleaning Service												29.68
Construction of Residential Complex												85.55
Dreadging Service												26.00
Mailing List Compilation & Mailing@												2.37
Club or Association												19.65
Packing Service@												3.59
Survey and Map Making@												2.62
Transport of goods through pipeline												120.29

(Contd...)

Services	1994-95	1995-96	1996-97	1997-98	1998-99	1999-2000	2000-01	2001-02	2002-03	2003-04	2004-05	2005-06
Site Preparation												20.42
Misc								0.23		38.18	3.87	
Cess											186.94	451.13
Mechanical slaughter					0.85			2.11	0.05	0.00	0.00	0.00
Total	**410.61**	**846.16**	**1022.01**	**1515.9**	**1787.1**	**2071.83**	**2611.68**	**3305.44**	**4124.89**	**7889.97**	**14196.19**	**23052.94**

Source: Annual Performance Report 2005-06

#Services are included in Telecommunication services in the year 2007.

*Top ten revenue contributor services.

@ Bottom ten revenue contributor services.

$ Some services with wider scope.

TOP TEN REVENUE CONTRIBUTOR SERVICES

The services which have been included in this category are the three services on which the tax was initially imposed in the year 1994. Therefore, their record is of a longer period. Certain other services which come under this category have been brought under the tax net much later. However, on the basis of their revenue earning there is an indication of strong revenue potentiality. These are Telecommunication Services, Banking and Other Financial Services, Business Auxiliary Services, Goods Transport Agency, General Insurance Business, Insurance Auxiliary Services, Management, Maintenance and Repair, Stock Broker Services, Consulting Engineer Service and Commercial or Industrial Construction Services.

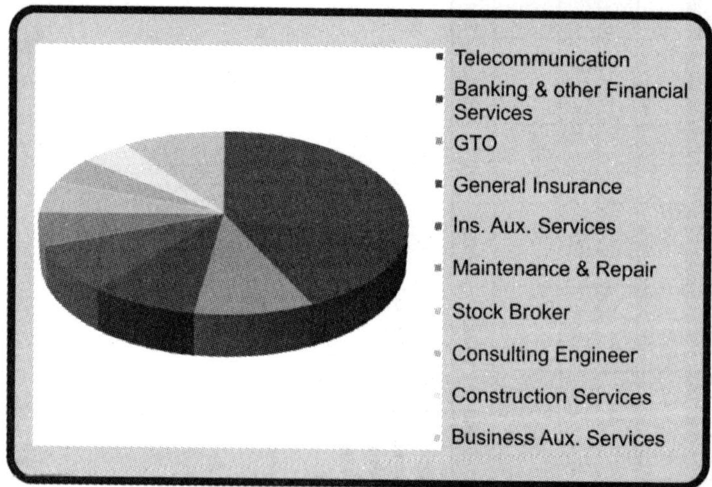

Fig. 5.1 : Top Ten Revenue Contributor Services

1. Telecommunication services: The revolutionary change in the field of information technology has brought the telecommunication services to the forefront. Telecommunication is a broad term and it comprehends a large number of services within its ambit. Initially clause

105 of Section 65 of The Finance Act, 1994 provided for separate heads of similar chargeable services. These six services were: Telephone (sub-clause b), Pager (sub-clause c), Telex (sub-clause zf), Fascimile (Fax) (sub-clause zg), Leased Circuit (sub-clause zd) and Telegraph (sub-clause ze) alongwith certain other similar services are now grouped into one larger head of 'Telecommunication Services'. The new provision of definition of telecommunication service is very exhaustive. As defined under the newly inserted[1] clause 109(a) it means:

> Telecommunication service of any description provided by means of any transmission, emission or reception of signs, signals, writing, images and sounds or intelligence or information of any nature, by wire, radio, optical, visual or other electro-magnetic means or systems, including the related transfer or assignment of the right to use capacity for such transmission, emission or reception by a person who has been granted a licence under the first proviso to sub-section(1) of section 4 of the Indian Telegraph act, 1885.

It includes

- Voice mail, data services, audio tax services, video tax services, radio paging;
- Fixed telephone services including provision of access to and of the public switched telephone network for the transmission and switching of voice, data and video inbound and out bound telephone service to and from national and international destinations;
- Cellular mobile telephone services including provision of access to and use of switched or non-switched networks for the transmission of voice, data and video, inbound and outbound roaming service to and from national and international destinations;
- Carrier services including provision of wired or wireless facilities to originate, terminate or transit calls, charging for interconnection, settlement or

termination of domestic or international calls, charging for jointly used facilities including pole attachments, charging for the exclusive use of circuits, a leased circuit or a dedicated link including a speech circuit, data circuit or a telegraph circuit;

- Provision of call management services for a fee including call waiting, call forwarding, caller identification, three-way calling, call display, call return, call screen, call blocking, automatic call-back, call answer, voice mall, voice menus and video conferencing;
- Private network services including provision of wired or wireless telecommunication link between specified points for the exclusive use of the client;
- Data transmission services including provisions of access to wire or wireless facilities and services specifically designed for efficient transmission of data; and
- Communication through facsimile, pager, telegraph and telex.

Does not include

- Any person in relation to on-line information and database access or retrieval or both referred to in sub-clause (zh) of clause(105);
- A broadcasting agency or organization in relation to broadcasting referred to in sub-clause (zk) of clause (105); and
- Any person in relation to internet telecommunication referred to in sub-clause (zzzu) of clause (105)

The above mentioned three services which are excluded here are as a matter of fact chargeable under separate heads.

Six major services were consolidated in 2007 in one broad category i.e. Telecommunication Services. While preparing the revenue table of the service we have considered all six services.

Table 5.2: Revenue Collection from Telecommunication Services

Financial Year	Revenue (Rs. Crores)	Percentage Growth
1994-95	202.05	Base year
1995-96	493.04	144.19
1996-97	586.03	18.32
1997-98	725.58	23.75
1998-99	847.28	16.77
1999-00	1197.08	41.37
2000-01	1155.95	-3.49
2001-02	1452.42	25.64
2002-03	1629.21	12.17
2003-04	2802.00	71.98
2004-05	4175.38	49.01
2005-06	4331.07	3.72

Source: Annual Performance Report 2005-06

The telecommunication service comprises one of the initially taxed service *i.e.* telephone services. The revenue receipt from this service is much higher than other services. In the very first year it is Rs. 202.05 crores next year it is increased to Rs. 493.4 crores and the growth rate was 144.19 per cent. In 1996-97 it includes pager service and the revenue receipt for this year was Rs. 586.30 crores. It shows continuous progress till the year 1999-2000. In 2000-01 the growth rate was negative it was (-)3.49 per cent. In the year 2001-02 it was comprised of four other services and the combined revenue receipts were Rs. 1452.42 crores and the growth rate was 25.64 per cent. In 2002-03 growth rate was

12.17 per cent, in 2003-04 it was 71.98 per cent, and in 2004-05 it was 49.01 per cent. In the year 2005-06 the revenue receipts is Rs. 4331.07 crores and the growth rate is 3.72 per cent. It accounted for 18.78 per cent of the total Service Tax revenue in the year 2005-06 and stood at the first position among of revenue receipts all services. This trend indicates the bright future from this head.

2. Banking and other financial services: Globalization and Industrialization have a natural consequence of increasing the volume of financial transaction. The computerization is the key word for all economic activities. Financial exchanges are moving from cash to paperless transactions. Banks and other financial institutions play an active role in this field, as a variety of services are provided by such institutions. Considering the ever increasing volume of financial transactions there is an enormous scope for raising revenue through imposition of Service Tax. Such services were brought under the tax net in the year 2001.These services were defined under Section 65(12) of the Finance Act, time to time several aspects have been redefined and changed in the year 2006.

"Banking and other financial services" means:

(*a*) The following service provided by a banking company or a financial institution including a non-banking financial company or any other body corporate or [any other person][2] namely:

(*i*) Financial leasing services including equipment leasing and hire purchase;

[3][**Explanation**—For the purpose of this item, 'financial leasing' means a lease transaction where—

(*a*) contract for lease is entered into between two parties for leasing of a specific asset;

(*b*) such contract is for use and occupation of the asset by the lessee;

(*c*) the lease payment is calculated so as to cover the full cost of the asset together with the interest charges; and

(*d*) the lessee is entitled to own, or has the option to own, the asset at the end of the lease period after making the lease payment;

[(*ii*) * * * *][4]

(*iii*) Merchant banking services;

(*iv*) Securities and foreign exchange (forex) broking;

(*v*) Asset management including portfolio management, all forms of fund management, pension fund management, custodial, depository and trust services, but does not include cash management;

(*vi*) Advisory and other auxiliary financial services including investment and portfolio research and advice, advice on mergers and acquisition and advice on corporate restructuring and strategy;

(*vii*) Provision and transfer of information and data processing; and

(*viii*) Banker to an issue services; and

(*ix*) Other financial services namely, lending issue of pay order, demand draft, cheque, letter of credit and bill of exchange, transfer of money including telegraphic transfer, mail transfer and electronic transfer, providing bank guarantee, overdraft facility, bill discounting facility, safe deposit locker, safe vaults; operation of bank accounts;

(*a*) Foreign exchange broking provided but a foreign exchange broker other than those covered under sub-clause (a);

Table 5.3 : Revenue Collection From Banking and Other Financial Services

Financial Year	Revenue (Rs. Crores)	Percentage Growth
2001-02	44.07	Base year
2002-03	174.56	290.51
2003-04	307.65	76.24
2004-05	1046.78	240.25
2005-06	1953.76	86.64

Source: Annual Performance Report 2005-06

The available data of revenue collection from 2001-02 to 2005-06 shows a steady increase. The amount of collection moved from meager Rs. 44.70 crores to Rs.174.56 crores that is four times increase. It amounts to 290.51 per cent growth of revenue in one year. The next year it was 76.24 per cent, in the third year it rose by 240.25 per cent and in the fourth year it became 86.64 per cent. Considering the average growth rate of the revenue for the five years from this head is 8.54 per cent. In 2005-06 it was accounted 8.48 per cent of the total Service Tax revenue. In future it would be the most lucrative head of Service Tax.

3. Business auxiliary services: In modern times due to the effect of specialization, business concerns are taking the help of other specialized services from other concerns *e.g.*. These services are grouped for the purposes of Service Tax under the head of 'Business Auxiliary Services'. In the recent past this sector is flourishing at a fast speed, covering several activities. These services were brought under the Service Tax net from 1.7.2003. The term 'Business Auxiliary Service' was defined in the Section 65(19) of the Finance Act, 1994. It was amended in 2004, 2005 and 2006. It is exhaustively covers a variety of such services. Under this definitional clause

'Business Auxiliary Service'[5] means any service in relation to—

(*i*) Promotion or marketing or sale of goods produced or provided by or on belonging to the client; or

(*ii*) Promotion or marketing of service provided by the client; or

(*iii*) Any customer care service provided on behalf of the client; or

(*iv*) Procurement of goods or services, which are input for the client; or

[**Explanation**- For the removal of doubts, it is hereby declared that for the purpose of this sub-clause, 'inputs' means all goods or services intended for use by the client][6]

[(*v*) Production or processing of goods for, or on behalf of, the client;][7]

(*vi*) Provision of service on behalf of the client; or

(*vii*) A service incidental or auxiliary to any activity specified in sub-clause(*i*) to (*vi*), such as billing, issue or collection or recovery of cheques, payments, maintenance of accounts and remittance, inventory management, evaluation or development of prospective customer or vendor, public relation services, management or supervision,

And includes services as a commission agent, but does not include any information technology service and any activity that amounts to 'manufacturer' within the meaning of clause (f) of section 2 of the Central Excise Act,1944(1 of 1944).

The revenue realized in the very first year was Rs. 49.80 crores and in the next year there was a spectacular growth in the revenue to the extent of 958.67 per cent over the year and in the next year the growth was 178.9 per cent over the last year. This indicates a vast potential of Service Tax revenue through this head of service.

Table 5.4: Revenue Collection from Business Auxiliary Services

Financial Year	Revenue (Rs. Crores)	Percentage Growth
2003-04	49.80	Base year
2004-05	527.22	958.61
2005-06	1470.44	178.09

Source: Annual Performance Report 2005-06

4. Goods transport agency: With the expansion of economic activity in various directions the transport services also proliferated. The increased quantity of goods are required to be transported from the place of the manufacture to the wholesaler and then to the retailer at far away places. Growth of this sector also gives an opportunity to impose Service Tax on the goods transport services. These services were brought under the Service Tax net in the year 1997. But due to the strike of the transporters it was withdrawn in

Table 5.5 : Revenue Collection from Goods Transport Agency

Financial Year	Revenue (Rs. Crores)	Percentage Growth
1997-98	73.85	Base year
1998-99	72.45	-1.89
1999-00	-14.52	-120.04
2000-01	24.58	
2001-02	6.75	-72.53
2002-03	5.13	-24.00
2003-04	0.00	0.00
2004-05	174.01	174.00
2005-06	1396.37	702.05

Source: Annual Performance Report 2005-06

1998. In the year 2004 it was re-introduced and again came under the tax ambit. Thus the effective date was 2.12.2004. The term 'Goods Transport Agency' has been defined under section 65(50b) of the Act.

> '*Goods Transport Agency*' means [any person][8] who provides services in relation to transport of goods by road and issues consignment note, by whatever name called.

The table 5.5 indicates that this service have great potentiality of revenue in the very first year was Rs.73.85 crores. After that it was started to decline due to the withdrawal of the tax on particular service. It was reintroduced in the year 2004 and that year the collection was Rs.174.1 crores in the very next year it was increased to Rs.1396.37 crores and shows a tremendous growth of 702.05 per cent. It accounted for 6.05 per cent of the total Service Tax receipt for the year 2005-06.

5. General insurance business: General insurance business is another fast growing sector of the developing economy like India. It is a segment of the growing infrastructure development.

> 'General Insurance business' has the meaning assigned to it in clause (g) of Section 3 of the General Insurance Business (Nationalization) Act, 1972(57 of 1972).

According to the said sub-clause (9) c, general insurance business includes:

- Fire insurance business
- Marine insurance business
- Miscellaneous insurance business

Does not include:

- Capital redemption business
- Annuity business

Table 5.6 : Revenue Collection from General Insurance Business

Financial Year	Revenue (Rs. Crores)	Percentage Growth
1994-95	173.11	Base year
1995-96	308.38	78.14
1996-97	355.04	15.13
1997-98	379.15	6.79
1998-99	405.08	6.83
1999-00	351.31	-13.27
2000-01	472.95	34.62
2001-02	553.07	17.07
2002-03	644.49	16.39
2003-04	1039.58	67.30
2004-05	1260.52	21.25
2005-06	1253.98	-0.51

Source: Annual Performance Report 2005-06

General Insurance Business Services are one among the three services on which tax was imposed initially in the year 1994-95. At that time the revenue collection from the service was Rs. 173.11 crores which increased to Rs. 308.38 crores in the next year and accounted to 78.14 per cent growth. In the year 1997-98 it was 6.80 per cent that indicated the potentiality of service. But in very next year *i.e.* in 1999-2000 the growth rate was negative and it was (-)13.27 per cent. Again in the year 2000-01 the revenue collection were rose and accounted for 34.62 per cent growth rate and then continuously the revenue collection were increasing it was increased to Rs. 553.70 crores in 2001-02 to Rs. 644.49 crores in 2002-03, Rs. 1039.58 crores in 2003-04, Rs. 1260.52 crores in 2004-05. There is little decline in the revenue collection in the year 2005-06 the growth rate was (-)0.51 per cent.

But still it accounted for 5.43 per cent of total Service Tax revenue and shows a great potentiality.

6. Insurance auxiliary services: These services were brought under the Service Tax net in the year 2001 at that time it included the auxiliary service in relation to only general insurance. The scope of the service has been expanded by including auxiliary service in relation to life insurance as well in the year 2002. As per Section 65 (55) of the Finance Act, 1994 the term

'Insurance auxiliary service' means any service provided by:

- An actuary;
- An intermediary; or
- Insurance intermediary; or
- An insurance agent in relation to general insurance business or life insurance business;
- Includes risk assessment;
- Claim settlement;
- Survey; and
- Loss assessment.

Table 5.7: Revenue Collection from Insurance Auxiliary Services

Financial Year	Revenue (Rs. Crores)	Percentage Growth
2001-02	34.24	Base Year
2002-03	104.83	206.16
2003-04	273.43	160.83
2004-05	713.29	160.86
2005-06	1216.17	70.50

***Source*:** Annual Performance Report 2005-06

The revenue collection from this service is Rs.1216.17 crores in the year 2005-06 it accounted for 5.28 per cent of total Service Tax revenue. The average revenue growth rate from the service is 690.38 per cent. It shows that in future it will be the major revenue contributor service.

7. Management, Maintenance and Repair: A necessary consequence of industrialization is that it led to increased in volume of durable machinery. The services under this head may be in the form of movable or immovable goods. During the course of time machineries require proper maintenance and repair for their optimum use and efficiency. This trend has given rise in number of various centers for providing a variety of services for management, maintenance and repair of such machineries and equipments. Such services are brought into the net of Service Tax from the year 2003-04.

As per section 65(64),

'Management maintenance or repair' means any service provided by—

(*i*) Any person under a contract or an agreement; or

(*ii*) A manufacturer or any person authorized by him, in relation to—

(*a*) Management of properties, whether immovable or not;

(*b*) Maintenance or repair of properties, whether immovable or not; or

(*c*) Maintenance or repair including reconditioning or restoration, or servicing of any goods, excluding a motor vehicle;

[**Explanation**—for the removable of doubts, it is hereby declared that for the purpose of this clause, "goods" includes computer software;][10]

The revenue collection for the first year was Rs.90.59 crores but in very next year it rose by 278 percent and revenue was Rs.342.43 crores and in the next year again it rose by

151 per cent and increase to Rs. 862.61 crores. This shows that it is one of the most lucrative sources of Service Tax revenue.

Table 5.8: Revenue Collection from Management, Maintenance or Repair

Financial Year	Revenue (Rs. Crores)	Percentage Growth
2003-04	90.59	Base year
2004-05	342.43	278
2005-06	862.61	151

Source**:** Annual Performance Report 2005-06

8. Stock Broker services: The processes of liberalization and privatization initiated in 1991 have shown a gradual improvement and development in the share market activities. Share market is the nerve-centre of modern economic life. Stock broker services were among the first three services brought under the tax net along with telephone and general insurance in the year 1994. Stock broker services provided by a stock broker to a person in connection with the sale or purchase of securities listed on a recognized stock exchange. The value of taxable service provided by a stock broker is the gross amount charged by the stock broker for the services rendered to an investor in connection with the sale or purchase of securities and includes the commission or brokerage paid by him to any sub-broker. As per Section 65(101),

'*Stock Broker*'[11] means a person who has either made an application for registration or is registered as a stock-broker or sub-broker as the case may be, in accordance with the rules and regulations made under the Securities and Exchange Board of India Act, 1992.

The revenue collections from stock broker services were increased from Rs.35.45 crores in 1994-95 to Rs. 823.57 crores in 2005-06. Except in the year 2002-03 it can be observed that it decreased to Rs.101.23 crores from Rs.280.76 crores in 2001-02. The growth rate from service is 119.09 per cent in 2005-06 over its earlier year. It was accounted to 3.57 per cent over the Service Tax revenue for the year 2005-06. There is a steady rise in the revenue and growth percentage from year to year.

Table 5.9: Revenue Collection from Stock Broker Services

Financial Year	Revenue (Rs. Crores)	Percentage Growth
1994-95	35.45	Base year
1995-96	44.38	25.19
1996-97	50.75	14.35
1997-98	55.95	10.24
1998-99	66.48	18.82
1999-00	185.62	179.21
2000-01	282.24	52.05
2001-02	280.76	-0.52
2002-03	101.23	-63.94
2003-04	249.99	146.95
2004-05	375.89	50.36
2005-06	823.57	119.09

Source: Annual Performance Report 2005-06

9. **Consulting engineer service:** In an expanding economy the consultancy activities e.g. consulting engineer, charted accountant, cost accountant, company secretary, architect, lawyer, doctors etc. are in great demand. Consulting engineer is the person or any firm which involve in rendering technical assistance or advice. These services were brought under the tax net in the 1997. The term consulting engineer has been defined under section 65(31).

"*Consulting Engineer* means any professionally qualified engineer or [any body corporate or any other firm] who, either directly or indirectly, renders any advice, consultancy or technical assistance in any manner to a client in one or more disciplines of engineering."

It includes the following category of services:

- Feasibility study;
- Pre-design service/project report;
- Basic design engineering;
- Detailed design engineering;
- Procurement;
- Construction, supervision and project management;
- Supervision of commissioning and initial operation;
- Manpower planning and training;
- Post-operation and management; and
- Trouble shooting and technical services including establishing systems and procedure for an existing plan.

It does not include

- Scientific and technical consultancy

According to Table 5.10 the revenue collection from this service is Rs.724.89 crores in the 2005-06 and accounted 3.4 per cent of total Service Tax revenue. The percentage growth for the first year 1998-99 was 121.5 per cent it indicates that in the very beginning it is one of the major source of Service Tax revenue. However, the revenue fell down to Rs. 47.97 crores that shows the sudden fall due to sluggishness in economy, political instability, administrative inefficiency and consequently inefficiency in the administration. However, the condition improves and again in the next year the growth was recorded 121 per cent. Once again there was a little stagnation in 2001-02. Thereafter 2002-03 to 2005-06 we find a continuous steep rise in the growth rate of revenue each year. However the present figure of revenue is Rs.724.89 crores shows an encouraging 9 years performance of the service and ranked at 9th position among all services.

Table 5.10: Revenue Collection from Consulting Engineer Services

Financial Year	Revenue (Rs. Crores)	Percentage Growth
1997-98	37.93	Base Year
1998-99	84.01	121.5
1999-00	43.97	-47.7
2000-01	97.18	121.0
2001-02	94.47	-2.78
2002-03	148.15	56.8
2003-04	280.68	89.4
2004-05	469.72	67.3
2005-06	724.89	54.3

Source: Annual Performance Report 2005-06

10. Commercial or Industrial Construction Services: Economic development also requires rapid industrialization which has given a boost to the commercial and industrial construction services. Construction is a wider phenomenon it covers wide range of different activities such as construction of roads, airport, railway, bridges and dams etc. All the Commercial construction services brought come under the Service Tax net from 2004. Initially it included charge was in respect of only commercial construction services but later on in the very next year industrial construction services were added in its ambit. Section 65(25 b) of the Act defines

'Commercial and industrial construction service' means:

(*a*) Construction of a new building or a civil structure or a part thereof; or (*b*) Construction of pipeline or conduit; or

(*c*) Completion and finishing services such as glazing, plastering, painting, floor and wall tiling, wall covering and wall papering, wood and metal joinery and carpentry, fencing and railing, construction of swimming pools, acoustic application or fittings and other similar services, in relation to building or civil structure; or

(*d*) Repair, alteration, renovation or restoration of, or similar services in relation to building or civil structure, pipeline or conduit, Which is—

(*i*) Used, or to be used, primarily for; or

(*ii*) Occupied, or to be occupied, primarily with; or engaged, or to be engaged, primarily in;

(*iii*) Engaged, or to be engaged, primarily in Commerce or industry, or work intended for commerce or industry, but does not include such services provided in respect of roads, airports, railways, transport terminals, bridges, tunnels and dams.

The revenue collection from construction services shows very rapid increase, it has increased 8 times within a year from Rs. 85.96 crores in 2004-05 to Rs. 663.24 crores in 2005-06. It was accounted 2.88 per cent of the total Service Tax revenue. The growth rates of the service are 671.56 per cent. As a matter of fact this is due to the widening of base as industrial construction is also added.

BOTTOM TEN REVENUE CONTRIBUTOR SERVICES

Under this category most of the services are newly introduced. Therefore, there available record of earning is only for a very short period. However they also have a good future prospect from the point of view of revenue. These are Opinion Poll Services, Mailing List Compilation, Survey and Map Making, Underwriter's Agency Services, Packing

Services, Cost Account Services, Travel Agents Services (Excluding travel by air or rail), Rail Travel Agent, Fashion Designer Service and Credit Rating Agency.

1. Opinion poll services: With the development of democratic institution and the role of media there is a sudden crop up of opinion poll agencies especially after the process of Liberalization was introduced. Service Tax is imposed on the agency providing the services of opinion poll. Both the term opinion poll and opinion poll agency are defined by law.

As per section 65(75a)[12]

> '*Opinion poll*' means any service designed to secure information on public opinion regarding social, economic, political or other issues.

As per section 65(75b)

> '*Opinion poll agency*' means any person engaged in providing any service in relation to opinion poll. These agencies are responsible for the payment of the tax.

These services were brought under the tax ambit in the year 2004. In the year 2005-06, amongst all the services the revenue collection from opinion poll services were the least and it was only Rs. 0.79 crores. However, the revenue is just double over the last years receipt *i.e.* 0.40 crores. But still it accounted for 0.0034 per cent of total Service Tax revenue.

2. Mailing List Compilation: Another important service which is gradually expanding and has a great potential from Service Tax is Mailing List Compilation. Service provided to any person, by any other person, in relation to mailing list compilation and mailing has also been brought in the tax net in the year 2005. As per section 65(63a)[13]

> 'Mailing list compilation and mailing means any service in relation to:

(*i*) Compiling and providing list of name, address and any other information from any source; or

(*ii*) Sending document, information, goods or any other material in a packet, by whatever name it is called, by addressing, stuffing, sealing, metering or mailing for or on behalf of the client.

Only one year data of mailing list compilation is available. This head received Rs.2.37 crores in the year 2005-06. Although the revenue collection amount is to only 0.010 per cent of total Service Provider revenue. The future prospect of increase in revenue under this head is bright.

3. Survey and Map Making: Survey and Map Making services are also growing with the policy of Privatization infrastructure development. Services provided to any person, by any other person, other than by an agency under the control of or authorized by the Government in relation to Survey and Map Making. These services were brought under the tax net in the year 2005. As per section 65(104b),

> '*Survey and map making*'[14] means geological, geophysical or any other prospecting, surface, sub-surface or aerial surveying or map-making of any kind, but does not include survey and exploration of mineral."

Revenue collection from Survey and map making services were Rs. 2.62 crores in the year 2005-06. These services accounted for 0.11 per cent of total Service Tax revenue.

4. Underwriter's Agency Services: With the increasing commercial transactions and corporate activities underwriting services are also in great need. The terms 'underwriter' and 'underwriting' both are defined in Section 65 (116 and 117) respectively. However, these terms are directly concerned with the provision of SEBI. Therefore, the definition given in Rule 2(f) and (g) of SEBI are given has been made applicable. These services were brought under the tax net in the year 1998.

Table 5.11: Revenue Collection from Underwriter Services

Financial Year	Revenue (Rs. Crores)	Percentage Growth
1998-99	0.01	Base year
1999-00	0.33	3200.00
2000-01	1.79	446.42
2001-02	2.21	23.46
2002-03	2.50	13.12
2003-04	2.17	-13.02
2004-05	1.08	-50.23
2005-06	3.38	212.96

Source: Annual Performance Report 2005-06

The revenue collection from this head is satisfactory. In the beginning it was only Rs.0.01crore but in the very next year it's increased to Rs.0.33 crores. Therefore, there is ample scope of revenue increase of this service through the efficient administrative control.

5. Packing Service: With the rise of the industrial and manufacturing sector and modernization there is a large scope for the packing material and methods services. Packing services are bound to proliferete. These services were brought under the Service Tax net in the year 2005. As per Section 65(76) 'packing activity' means

Packaging of goods including pouch filling, bottling, labeling or imprinting of the package, but does not include any packaging activity that amounts to manufacture within the meaning of clause (f) of section 2 of the Central Excise Act, 1944 (1 of 1944).[15]

The revenue collection was Rs. 3.59 crores in the year 2005-06 which was accounted 0.01 per cent of the total Service Tax revenue. With the efficient tax administration there appears to be every possibility of getting more revenue under this head.

6. *Cost Account Services*: The cost accountant services are increasing day by day with the economic activities. These services were brought under the tax ambit in the year 1998. The term 'Practising Cost Accountant' has been defined in Section 65 (84) of the Finance Act

'*Practising Cost Accountant*' means a person who is a member of the institute of Cost and works accountant of India and is holding a certificate of practice granted under the provisions of the Cost and Works Accountants Act,1980 (23 of 1959) and includes any concern engaged in rendering services in the field of cost accountancy.

Table 5.12: Revenue Collection from Cost Accountant Services

Financial Year	Revenue (Rs. Crores)	Percentage Growth
1998-99	0.06	Base year
1999-00	0.27	350.00
2000-01	0.35	29.62
2001-02	0.35	0.00
2002-03	1.22	174.00
2003-04	1.08	-11.47
2004-05	1.93	78.70
2005-06	4.47	131.60

Source: Annual Performance Report 2005-06

The revenue collection from the service is increasing continuously it was Rs.0.06 crores in the year 1998-99 which increased to Rs.0.27 crores in the very next year and recorded 350.00 per cent growth in the first year. Though in the second year revenue were increased to Rs. 0.35 crores but the growth rate was only 29.62 per cent in the third year the growth rate was stagnant in the fourth year was again recorded a tremendous increase with the growth rate of 174.00 per cent in the next year *i.e.* the fifth year it was (-) 11.47 per cent this decrement was due to political instability and inefficiency in administration. In 2004-05 it was 78.70 per cent growth and in the year 2005-06 it is 131.60 per cent and accounted for 0.019 per cent of the total tax revenue. The trend of revenue collection indicates that though not very satisfactory but it has a good prospect in future.

7. Travel Agents Services (Excluding travel by air or rail): With the increase in population and economic activities travelling by rail, air and road have also increased. A number of travelling agencies are providing a number of facilities related to travelling such as booking, cancelation and connecting services *etc.*. These services were brought under the tax net in the year 2004. As per Section 65 (115a)

> 'A travel agent' means any person engaged in providing any service connected with booking of passage for travel, but does not includes air travel agent and rail travel agent.

The revenue collection from this service shows tremendous growth within two years it was Rs.2.82 crores in 2004-05 which increased to Rs.6.14 crores in 2005-06. The growth rate was 117.73 per cent which shows the potentiality of the service in future.

8. Rail Travel Agent: In modern fast life the service of rail travel agent are frequently used. Therefore such services are also brought under the tax net in 2002. As per section 65(87)

> '*Rail Travel Agent*' means any person engaged in providing any service connected with booking of passage for travel by rail.

The services must be associated with the booking of passage for travel by rail only. Any other ancillary services provided by rail travel agent to its customers such as booking of hotel, arrangement of local transport booking of luggage should not be included under this head. All rail travel agents whether registered or unregistered are come under the tax net.

Table 5.13: Revenue Collection from Rail Travel Agent

Financial Year	Revenue (Rs. Crores)	Percentage Growth
2002-03	0.69	Base year
2003-04	2.03	194.20
2004-05	4.17	105.41
2005-06	6.20	48.68

Source: Annual Performance Report 2005-06

The revenue collection was Rs. 0.69 crores in 2002-03 which increased to Rs.2.03 crores in next year and accounted for 194.20 per cent growth. The revenue was increased to Rs. 4.17 crores in 2004-05 and again to Rs. 6.20 crores in 2005-06. It was accounted for 0.026 per cent of the total Service Tax revenue.

9. Fashion Designer Service: Socio-economic development raises the standard of living of the people both of rural and urban areas. Globalization has also helped in the interaction of cross-culture leading towards greater demand of fashion designer services. The growth in electronic media and print media especially T.V. has further effects the growth of fashion designing industry. With the widening scope of the service these services were brought under the tax net in 2002. Both the term 'Fashion Designing' and 'Fashion Designer' are defined in the Act in the Section 65 (43 and 44) respectively.

'Fashion Designing' includes

Any activity relating top patterns for costumes, apparels, garments, clothing accessories, jewellery or any other articles intended to be worn by human beings and any other service incidental thereto.

'Fashion Designers' means

Any person engaged in providing service in relation to fashion designing.

Fashion Designing includes any activities relating to

- Conceptualizing
- Outlining
- Creating the designs and preparing patterns for customers

It does not include:

- Stitching of clothes by tailor;
- Making of jewellery by the jeweler;
- Garment making

Table 5.14: Revenue Collection from Fashion Designer Service

Financial Year	Revenue (Rs. Crores)	Percentage Growth
2002-03	0.46	Base year
2003-04	1.46	217.39
2004-05	8.13	456.84
2005-06	6.44	-20.78

Source: Annual Performance Report 2005-06

The trend of revenue of four years period shows a disturbing trend. Though the second year the revenue was encouraging as it tripled from the preceding year. In the next *i.e.* the third year it was about eight times and the growth rate was 217.3 per cent. The down fall in the fourth year indicates the lack of administrative efficiency in handling this sector.

10. Credit Rating Agency: Credit Rating Agency determines the financial ability and credit worthiness of a person to determine its ability to raise credit from the market or financial institution. These agencies provide gradation of credit worthiness of a person or business. The main purposes of these agencies are to ensure that the investor is aware of the relative safety of the amount invested by him. These agencies are registered with the Reserve Bank of India and provide rating in respect of corporate bonds, utilities, assets, debt structural obligation, mutual funds *etc.*. These services were brought under the Service Tax net on 16.10.1998. The term has been defined under Section 65 (34) of the Act.

> '*Credit Rating Agency*' means [any person][16] engaged in the business of credit rating of any debt obligation or of any project or programme, requiring finance, whether in the form of debt or otherwise, and includes credit rating of any financial obligation, instrument or security, which has the purpose of providing a potential investor or any other person any information pertaining to relative safety of payment of interest or principal.

Table 5.15: Revenue Collection from Credit Rating Agency

Financial Year	Revenue (Rs. Crores)	Percentage Growth
1998-99	0.57	Base year
1999-00	1.79	214.03
2000-01	2.56	43.01
2001-02	3.69	44.14
2002-03	11.26	205.14
2003-04	13.14	16.69
2004-05	11.63	-11.49
2005-06	13.03	12.03

Source: Annual Performance Report 2005-06

The credit rating agency services are at 10th position among bottom ten services. But this head indicated very much scope in future. The growth was 214.03 per cent in 1999-2000 that declined to 43.01 per cent in 2000-01. The growth rate was negative in the year 2004-05. But again in the next year 2005-06 it was raised to 12.03 per cent and accounted for 0.05 per cent of the total Service Tax revenue.

SOME SERVICES WITH WIDER SCOPE

Services included in this category are brought under the tax net at a later stage but there earning is substantial from the very beginning. Thus, they are more promising revenue earner for the future. These are Advertising Services, Broadcasting Services, Courier Service, Security Agency, Port Services, Chartered Accountants Service, Clearing and Forwarding Agent, Erection Commissioning and Installation Services, Airport Services and Commercial Coaching Centers and Tutorials Services.

1. Advertising Services: Advertising agency business is a flourishing sector. Besides other services its contribution is bound to increase with the growth of print and electronic media. Advertisement is a means of public announcement. Advertising is a form of communication intended to promote the sale of a product or service, to influence public opinion, to gain political support, to advance a particular cause, or to elicit some other response desire by the advertiser. Service tax on advertising agency was imposed on 1.11.1996.

As per Section 65(2), 'Advertisement' includes:

> Any notice, circular, label, wrapper, document, hoarding or any other audio or sound, smoke or gas.

As per Section 65(3), 'Advertising agency' means

> Any [person][17] engaged in providing any service connected with the making, preparation, display or exhibition of advertisement and includes an advertising consultant.

The following types of services shall be included:

- Advertising agency
- Advertisement consultant
- Film produces directly charging to client

- Person engaged in transferring audio-visual representation from one mode to another
- Printing press making advertisement and billing to the client
- Computer typesetters making the advertisement and directly billing to client
- Artist making advertisement and directly billing to client
- Models working for advertisement and directly billing to client
- Person engaged in window display of advertisement and charging to client directly
- Display board at railway station, airports, public places, etc. and charging directly to clients.
- Person owing neon sign boards for displaying advertisement and charging directly to client
- Person displaying the advertisement in play ground at the time of matches etc. and charging rent directly from client.

The following shall not be included:

- Department of Audio and Visual Publicity (DAVP)
- Person engaged in creating specialized data base
- Charitable institution
- Canvassing of advertisement i.e. space selling for advertisement
- Publication of telephone directories or yellow pages
- Newspaper and journals
- Cinema theatres like PVR, Metro etc.

The table shows the steady growth of revenue collection from advertising agency services and it shows a great potential as well. A decade's period of revenue earning is very encouraging and during this period the average growth rate is 215.87 per cent. The revenue earning was jumped from Rs. 19.33 crores in 1996-97 to Rs. 136.62 crores.

Table 5.16: Revenue Collection from Advertising Agency Service

Financial Year	Revenue (Rs. Crores)	Percentage Growth
1996-97	19.33	Base year
1997-98	89.75	364.30
1998-99	89.73	-0.02
1999-00	86.18	-3.95
2000-01	110.47	28.18
2001-02	150.18	35.94
2002-03	174.73	16.34
2003-04	220.29	26.07
2004-05	351.80	59.69
2005-06	436.62	24.11

Source: Annual Performance Report 2005-06

2. **Broadcasting Services:** The era of New Economic Reform started in 1991 have widened the scope of broadcasting services. T.V. and radio is the vehicle of growth in this field. Entertainment through serials, sports and educational services have raised the demand for broadcasting services both at national and international level. Increasing number of channels of regional languages and the demand for international channels have given a definite boost to the broadcasting business. Service tax on broadcasting services was imposed from 16-7-2001. All the broadcasting agencies or organizations are responsible for the payment of Service Tax. As per section 65(15)

Broadcasting as to have the meaning assigned to it in Clause(c) of section 2 of Prasar Bharti (Broadcasting Corporation of India) Act,1990 (25 of 1990) and also includes programme selection, scheduling or presentation of sound or visual matter on a radio or television channel that is intended for public listening or viewing, as the case may be, and in the case of broadcasting organization or agency, having its head office situated in any place outside India, includes the activity of selling of time slots or obtaining sponsorship for broadcasting of any programme or [collecting broadcasting charges or permitting the rights to picture, image and sounds of all kinds by transmission of electro magnetic waves through space or through cables, direct to home signals or by any other person on behalf of the said agency][18] or organization by its branch office or subsidiary or representative in India or any agent appointed in India or any person who act on his behalf in any manner.

Table 5.17: Revenue Collection From Broadcasting Services

Financial Year	Revenue (Rs. Crores)	Percentage Growth
2001-02	13.25	Base year
2002-03	90.45	582.64
2003-04	177.48	96.21
2004-05	272.95	53.79
2005-06	415.27	52.14

Source: Annual Performance Report 2005-06

The revenue collection from this service indicates high level of potentiality. In the very first year 2001-02 it was Rs. 13.25 crores which increased to Rs.90.45 crores in the next year and recorded 582.64 percent annual growth. In the very next year the growth rate was 96.21 per cent and the revenue collection was Rs. 177.48 crores. In the year 2004-05 it's again increase to Rs. 272.95 crores and percentage growth was 52.39 per cent. In the year 2005-06 the growth percentage was 52.14 per cent which depicts that there is a great potentiality from this head in future.

3. **Courier service**: Information and communication is the sine-qua-non for the growth and overall economic development of any society. The agency providing Courier Services are fulfilling a very valuable task in this direction. Courier services provided the facility of speedy communication. It is important not only for trade and commerce but also helping the common man. Such services are in great demand and scope of Service Tax in this sector is definitely widening. These services were brought under the tax net from 1996.

As per section 65(33)

> '*Courier Agency*' means a [any person][19] engaged in the door -to-door transportation of time-sensitive documents, goods or articles utilizing the services of a person, either directly or indirectly to carry or accompany such documents, goods or article.

'Express Cargo Service' transporters are not different from the courier. The following shall be included:

- Courier Agencies;
- Angadias;
- Value paid parcel services by courier agency.

The following shall not be included:

- Express / Lorry Services;
- Containers/Lorry Services;
- Co-loaders.

The revenue trend from this service shows great potentiality and accounted for 1.63 per cent of the total Service Tax revenue for the year 2005-06. With available data of a decade it is evident that there was positive growth rate throughout the decade except for two year *i.e.*1998-99 and 2005-06. In the very first year growth rate was recorded 356.09 percent and the revenue increased to Rs. 10.59 crores to Rs. 48.30 crores. Within a decade it jumped to Rs. 376.49 crores and the average growth rate was 345.51 per cent. All this trends indicates that the revenue from this head has bright scope in future.

Table 5.18: Revenue Collection From Courier Service

Financial Year	Revenue (Rs. Crores)	Percentage Growth
1996-97	10.59	Base year
1997-98	48.30	356.09
1998-99	45.84	-5.09
1999-00	63.43	38.37
2000-01	110.39	74.03
2001-02	111.62	1.11
2002-03	127.23	13.98
2003-04	227.01	78.42
2004-05	391.53	72.47
2005-06	376.49	-3.84

***Source*:** Annual Performance Report 2005-06

4. Security agency: Security Agencies are in great demand in every walk of life. Their need is felt not only in case of industrial houses but they are great demand in private houses as well as in multi storied buildings. These services were brought under the tax net in year 1998.

Section 65(94) of the Finance Act, 1995 defines

> *Security Agency* means any [person][20] engaged in the business of rendering services relating to the security of any property, whether movable or immovable, or of any person, in any manner and includes the services of investigation, detection or verification, of any fact or activity, whether of a personal nature or otherwise, including the services of providing security personnel.

Thus the ambit of the security agency is wide enough to include not only agencies rendering services of providing security but also detective agency services which are providing confidential services in respect of, say, financial credibility of any person, trademark, copyright, infringement *etc.*.

Table 5.19: Revenue Collection from Security Agency

Financial Year	Revenue (Rs. Crores)	Percentage Growth
1998-99	5.36	Base year
1999-00	13.93	159.88
2000-01	37.38	168.34
2001-02	40.88	9.36
2002-03	62.11	51.93
2003-04	118.02	90.01
2004-05	200.06	69.51
2005-06	308.10	54.00

Source: Annual Performance Report 2005-06

The revenue realized from this service in the very first year was Rs. 5.36 crores and show a spectacular growth of 159.88 per cent in 1999-2000, in the very next year it was recorded 168.34 per cent growth. In 2001-02 the growth rate was declined to 9.36 per cent. After that the growth rate was continuously rising and it was recorded more than 50 per cent for the next four year and indicates great revenue in future.

5. Port service: With the increasing economic activity port services are in great demand. Ports refer to a town or place possessing a harbor where ships load or unload or begin or end their voyages or at which passengers embark or disembark. Port services are brought into the tax net from 2001. The definition of Port Service has been given in the Section 65(82) of the Finance Act, 1994.

'*Port Service*' means any service rendered by a person or other port or any person authorized by such port or other port, in any manner, in relation to vessel or goods.

The following are included:

- Port Trust Authorities;
- Private companies providing port services;
- Gain service provider at port;
- Minor ports.

The following are not included:

- Airport Authority of India Ltd.;
- Land Custom Station;
- Inland Container Depots.

Table 5.20: Revenue Collection from Port Service

Financial Year	Revenue (Rs. Crores)	Percentage Growth
2001-02	90.26	Base year
2002-03	194.47	115.45
2003-04	359.45	84.83
2004-05	610.68	69.89
2005-06	654.30	7.14

Source: Annual Performance Report 2005-06

The revenue collection from this service is Rs. 90.26 crores in the year 2001-02 in the very next year it increased to Rs. 194.47 crores and the growth rate was 115.45 per cent. In second year the percentage growth was 84.83 per cent in the year 2004-05 it was 69.89 per cent. In the fifth year of its levy the revenue collection is Rs. 654.30 crores and the growth rate is 7.14 per cent. This shows that the revenue collection from this head of Service Tax is increasing rapidly and the average growth rate is 124.98 per cent. It was accounted for 2.83 per cent of the total Service Tax revenue. Evidently it indicates that there is a great future from this head.

6. Chartered Accountants Service: With the increase of various economic activities chartered accountants are playing active role in these activities. The service of practicing chartered accountant is brought under the Service Tax net in the year 1998.

As per Section 65(83)

> '*Practicing Chartered Accountant*' means a person who is the member of the institute of chartered accountant of India and is holding a certificate of practice granted under the provision of Chartered Accountants Act, 1949(38 of 1949) and includes any concern engaged in rendering services in the field of chartered accountancy.

Table 5.21: Revenue Collection from the Chartered Accountant Service

Financial Year	Revenue (Rs. Crores)	Percentage Growth
1998-99	2.80	Base year
1999-00	10.75	283.92
2000-01	37.13	245.39
2001-02	62.57	68.51
2002-03	74.60	19.22
2003-04	114.04	52.86
2004-05	187.91	64.77
2005-06	204.23	8.68

Source: Annual Performance Report 2005-06

In the year 1998-99 three professional services were brought under the tax net and one of them was Chartered Accounted Services. It recorded Rs. 2.80 crores revenue in the first year. In the very next year it rose to five times as compare to previous year. In the year 2000-01 its growth rate was 245.39 per cent and the revenue collection was Rs.37.13 crores, in 2001-02 it was Rs. 62.57 crores, in 2002-03 it was 74.60 crores, in the year 2003-04 again rose to Rs.114.04 crores, in 2004-05 it was Rs. 187.91 crores, in the year 2005-06 it was Rs. 204.23 crores. The trend shows that this head would became the major contributor in the revenue of Service Tax in the future.

7. Erection, Commissioning and Installation Services: with the ever increasing role of economic activities the use of various machinery or equipments are increasing and their installation and commissioning activities are also growing. Therefore there is great potentiality of taxing this area and they were brought under the Service Tax net in the year 2003. Through the Finance Act, 2004 the scope of commissioning and installation service has been widened to include 'Erection'.

As per Section 65(39a)

Erection Commissioning or installation means any service provided by commissioning and installation agency, in relation to,[21]

(*i*) Erection, commissioning or installation of plan, [machinery, equipment or structures, whether prefabricated or otherwise];[22] or

(*ii*) Installation of—

(*a*) Electrical and electronic devices, including wiring or fitting therefore; or

(*b*) Plumbing, drain laying or other installation for transport of fluids; or

(*c*) Heating, ventilation or air conditioning including related pipe work, duct work and sheet metal work; or

(*d*) Thermal insulation, sound insulation, fire proofing or water proofing; or

(*e*) Lift and escalator, fire escape, staircases or revelators; or

(*f*) Such other similar services.

Table 5.22: Revenue Collection from Erection Commissioning and Installation

Financial Year	Revenue (Rs. Crores)	Percentage Growth
2003-04	23.80	Base year
2004-05	137.50	477.73
2005-06	441.55	221.12

Source: Annual Performance Report 2005-06

The growth rate of revenue from this service was 477.73 per cent in the year 2004-05 and it again rises to 221.12 per cent in the year 2005-06. The revenue collection rose to Rs. 441.55 crores in 2005-06 from the meager amount of Rs. 23.80 crores in 2003-04 that indicates bright future prospects from this head.

8. Clearing and Forwarding Agent: With the passage of time various developmental activities are increasing rapidly and the role of different commission agents are coming in the forefront. For widening the tax base clearing and forwarding agents services have come into the Service Tax net in the year 1997. Section 65(25) of the Finance Act, 1994, defines such activities as:

> '*Clearing and Forwarding*' means any person who is engaged in providing any service either directly or indirectly connected with clearing and forwarding operations, in any manner to any other person and includes a consignment agent.

Thus, the clearing and forwarding agent is concerned with movement of goods. A manufacturer of any goods or even a dealer may engage a person to carry out clearing and forwarding either in the place of business or a remote place or a distribution centers.

According to Table 5.23 the revenue receipts from this head were Rs.19.13 crores in the first year. In the year 1998-99 the growth was 94.77 per cent, in the very next year the growth rate turned to negative and it was (-)49.32 per cent. In the year 2000-01 it's again rose and the growth rate turned to 176.69 per cent. In 2001-02 it was stagnant and in the year 2002-03 the growth rate was 13.18 per cent. After that in the year 2003-04 revenue receipt jumped from meager amount of Rs. 59.13 crores to huge amount of Rs. 118.41 crores. In the year 2004-05 the recorded growth was 50.42 per cent. In the year 2005-06 it was Rs. 209.80 and the growth rate is 17.78 per cent and accounted for 0.9100 per cent.

Table 5.23: Revenue Collection from Clearing and Forwarding Agents

Financial Year	Revenue (Rs. Crores)	Percentage Growth
1997-98	19.13	Base year
1998-99	37.26	94.77
1999-00	18.88	-49.32
2000-01	52.24	176.69
2001-02	52.24	0.00
2002-03	,59.13	13.18
2003-04	118.41	100.25
2004-05	178.12	50.42
2005-06	209.80	17.78

Source: Annual Performance Report 2005-06

9. Airport service: Globalization of the world economy opened various new sectors of development. Through this process the people are coming closer and world is becoming smaller place for us. Thus the air transport activities are increasing day-by-day. With the development of the sector the Airport Services were came under the tax net in the year 2004. Airport Service means the service provided by airport authority or any person authorize by it, in an airport or civil enclave to any person. The term aircraft, aircraft operator, airport and airport authority have been defined in Section 65 (3a),(3b),(3c) and (3d) respectively in the Finance Act,1994.

'Aircraft'[23] has the meaning assigned to it in clause (1) of section 2 of Aircraft Act, 1934 (22 of 1934);

'Aircraft Operator'[24] means any person who provides the service of transport of goods or passengers by aircraft;

'Airport' has the meaning assigned to it in clause (b) of section 2 of the Airport Authority of India Act, 1994(55 of 1994);

'Airport Authority' means the Airport Authority of India constituted under section 3 of the Airport Authority of India Act, 1994(55 of 1994) and also includes any person having the charge of management of an airport or a civil enclave.

The term civil enclave has also been defined in Finance Act, 1994 in section 65(24a) it has the meaning assigned to it in clause (b) of the Airport Authority Act, 1994.

Table 5.24: Revenue Collection from Airport Service

Financial Year	Revenue (Rs. Crores)	Percentage Growth
2004-05	58.56	Base year
2005-06	467.05	332.07

Source: Annual Performance Report 2005-06

The revenue collection data for two years is available of this particular service which indicates the growth rate of 467.05 percent and revenue were Rs. 58.56 crores in 2004-05 which grows to 332.07 in 2005-06. It was accounted for 2.02 per cent of the total Service Tax revenue in the year 2005-06.This indicates that this head of collecting revenue has a wider scope.

10. Commercial Coaching Centres and Tutorial Services: Training is an important task for the development of special skills and specialization in any profession. The purpose of coaching and tutorial classes is to brush up on basic skills, preparation for selective and independent examination etc. The basic aim of coaching and tutorial classes is to build-up skills, develop full potential of the client, improve motivation, concentration and confidence, achieve high academic standard, positive study skills, recommendation for appropriate personal development *etc.*. These services were brought under the tax net in the year 2003. Section 65 (26 and 27) have defined 'Commercial training or coaching' and 'commercial training or coaching centre' respectively in Finance Act, 1994.

> '*Commercial training or coaching*' means any training or coaching provided by a commercial training or coaching centre;
>
> '*Commercial training or coaching centre*' means any institute or establishment providing commercial training or coaching for imparting skill of knowledge or lessons on any subject or field other than the sports, with or without issuance of a certificate and includes coaching or tutorials classes but does not include preschool coaching and training centre or any institute or establishment which issues any certificate or diploma or degree or any educational qualification recognized by law for time being in force.

Table 5.25: Revenue Collection From Commercial Coaching Centre

Financial Year	Revenue (Rs. Crores)	Percentage Growth
2003-04	29.68	Base year
2004-05	109.75	269.77
2005-06	195.36	78.00

Source: Annual Performance Report 2005-06

The revenue collection from this service was Rs. 29.68 crores which increased to Rs. 109.75 crores and depicted a meager growth rate of 269.77 per cent. In the third year of its levy it was rose to Rs. 195.36 crores. This head was accounted for 0.78 per cent of the total Service Tax revenue.

The aforesaid analysis of selected thirty services reflects the high revenue potentiality of Service Tax, not only from these services but from the service sector in general. The trend is so encouraging that if up to date data of full fifteen year's is made available these findings will be further strengthened.

The four new services proposed to be added in the budget 2009-10 *viz.* Service provided in relation to transport of goods by rail, Service provided in relation to transport of coastal goods and goods through Inland Water including National Waterways, Legal consultancy service, Cosmetic and plastic surgery service indent are also expected to be a substantial source of revenue earning.

REFERENCES

1. Inserted (w.e.f.1.5.2006) by Section Finance Act, 2006
2. Substituted (w.e.f. 10-09-2007) by Section 135 of the Finance Act, 2007.
3. Inserted (w.e.f. 1-6-2007) by Section 135 of the Finance Act, 2007.
4. Omitted (w.e.f. 1-5-2006) by Section 68 of the Finance Act, 2006.
5. Substituted (w.e.f. 10-9-2004) by Section 90 of the Finance Act, 2004.
6. Inserted (w.e.f. 16-6-2005) by Section 88 of the Finance Act, 2005.
7. Substituted (w.e.f. 16-6-2005) by Section 88 of the Finance Act, 2005.
8. The definition was changed effective from 1.05.06 replacing the term 'commercial concern' by 'any person'
9. Sustituded (w.e.f.1.5.2006) by Section 68 of the Finance Act,2006.
10. Inserted (w.e.f. 1.6.2007) by Section 135 of the Finance Act, 2007.
11. Substituted (w.e.f.10.9.2004) by Section of the Finance Act, 2004.

12. Inserted (w.e.f. 10.9.2004) by Section 90 of the Finance Act, 2004.
13. Inserted (w.e.f. 16.6.2005) by Section 88 of the Finance Act, 2005
14. Inserted (w.e.f. 16.06.2005) by Section 88 of the Finance Act, 2005.
15. Inserted (w.e.f. 16.06.2005) by Section 88 of the Finance Act, 2005.
16. The term 'commercial concern' has been substituted by the term 'person' effective from 18.4.2006
17. The term 'commercial concern' is replaced by the term 'person' by the Finance Act, 2006, w.e.f. 1.5.2006.
18. Substituted (w.e.f. 16.6.2005) by Section 88 of the Finance Act, 2005
19. Substituted (w.e.f. 1.5.2006) by Section 68 of the Finance Act, 2006.
20. Substituted (w.e.f. 1.5.2006) by Section 68 of the Finance Act, 2006.
21. Substituted (w.e.f. 16.6.2005) by Section 88 of the Finance Act, 2005.
22. Substituted (w.e.f. 1.5.2006) by Section 68 of the Finance Act, 2006.
23. Inserted (w.e.f.10-9-2004) by Section 90 of the Finance (No. 2) Act, 2004.
24. Substituted(w.e.f.1-5-2006) by Section 68 of the Finance Act, 2006.

Goods and Service Tax in India

INTRODUCTION

In India, there exist a number of indirect taxes that are either levied by the Central or the State Government such as excise duty, custom duty, service tax, stamp duty, octroi and many more. There have been various or several attempts of reforming the indirect tax structure for making tax system simple stable and less burdensome. At federal level, efforts are being made to integrate taxes. The process of tax reform has already started in India. The indirect tax regime is undergoing a change and in the coming times the tax reforms will centre on an efficient and harmonized consumption tax system in country VAT at state level or CENVAT at the central level along with Service Tax have been major steps in tax reforms. Before the present tax regime, there was a cascading effect on tax, VAT has removed this burden, but it had deficiencies. The CENVAT load remains. There were several states taxes which were not subsumed in any one tax. The inter state sales tax or CST was not fully relieved. All this will be accomplished in the indirect tax system; GST will be the next logical step and a major breakthrough in the history of tax reforms in the country.

As a first major step in the GST direction the release of First Discussion Paper and Report of Task Force on GST are the major break. The second step is the need for constitutional amendment, as the power of levying Service Tax will be given to state, because it is a dual structure. To subsume, so many Acts we also require a constitutional amendment. The GST on imports will also require one. State Government has autonomy in selecting rates. In GST, the rates will be exactly the same, so it will be harmonious structure. If there is an exigency, or state have items of local importance or choice of the list of exempted items which do not effect inter state trade there will be given flexibility. All federal structures have faced the problem. We are going to take care of it through constitutional amendments.

WHAT IS GST?

The Goods and Service Tax (GST) is proposed to be a comprehensive indirect tax levy on manufacture, sale and consumption of goods as well as services at a national level. Integration of goods and services taxation would give India a world class tax system and improve tax collections. It would end the long standing distortions of differential treatments of manufacturing and service sector. The introduction of goods and services tax will lead to the abolition of taxes such as octroi, Central sales tax, State level sales tax, entry tax, stamp duty, telecom licence fees, turnover tax, tax on consumption or sale of electricity, taxes on transportation of goods and services, and eliminate the cascading effects of multiple layers of taxation. GST will facilitate seamless credit across the entire supply chain and across all states under a common tax base. Some of the salient features of GST in India are it Consistent with the federal structure of the country, the GST will have two components: one levied by the Centre (hereinafter referred to as Central GST), and the other levied by the States (hereinafter referred to as State GST). This dual GST model would be implemented through multiple statutes (one for CGST and SGST statute for every State). However, the basic features of law such as chargeability, definition of taxable event and taxable person, measure of levy including valuation provisions, basis of classification etc. would be uniform across these statutes as far as practicable. The Central GST and the State GST would be applicable to all transactions of goods and services except the exempted goods and services, goods which are outside the purview of GST and the transactions which are below the prescribed threshold limits. The Central GST and State GST are to be paid to the accounts of the Centre and the States separately. Since the Central GST and State GST are to be treated separately, in general, taxes paid against the Central GST shall be allowed to be taken as input tax credit (ITC) for the Central GST and could be utilized only against the payment of Central GST. The same principle will be applicable for the State GST. Cross utilization of ITC between the Central GST and the State GST would, in general, not be allowed. To the extent feasible, uniform procedure for collection of both Central GST and State GST would be prescribed in the respective legislation for Central GST and State GST. The administration of the Central GST would be with the Centre and for State GST with the States. The taxpayer would need to submit periodical returns to both the Central GST authority and to the concerned State GST authorities. Each taxpayer would be allotted a PAN-linked taxpayer identification number with a total of 13/15 digits. This would bring the GST PAN-linked system in line with the prevailing PAN-based system for Income tax facilitating data exchange and taxpayer compliance. The exact design would be worked out in consultation with the Income-Tax Department. Keeping in mind the need of tax payer's convenience, functions such as assessment, enforcement, scrutiny and audit would be undertaken by the authority which is collecting the tax, with information sharing between the Centre and the States.

The following taxes should be, subsumed under the Goods and Services

Tax:

Central Taxes	State Taxes
Central excise duty	Value Added Tax/ Sales tax
Additional excise duties	Entertainment tax (unless it is levied on local bodies)
Service tax	Luxury tax
Excise duty under Medicinal & Toiletries Preparation Act	Tax on lottery, betting and gambling
Countervailing duties (on imports in lieu of excise duty)	Entry tax not in lieu of Octroi
Additional duty of Customs (levied on imports in lieu of value added tax or central sales tax)	State surcharges and cesses in so far as they relate to supply of goods and services
Surcharges and Cesses	

JUSTIFICATION OF GST

Despite this success with VAT, there are still certain shortcomings in the structure of VAT both at the Central and at the State level. The shortcoming in CENVAT of the Government of India lies in non-inclusion of several Central taxes in the overall framework of CENVAT, such as additional customs duty, surcharges, etc., and thus keeping the benefits of comprehensive input tax and service tax set-off out of reach for manufacturers/ dealers. Moreover, no step has yet been taken to capture the value-added chain in the distribution trade below the manufacturing level in the existing scheme of CENVAT. The introduction of GST at the

Central level will not only include comprehensively more indirect Central taxes and integrate goods and service taxes for the purpose of set-off relief, but may also lead to revenue gain for the Centre through widening of the dealer base by capturing value addition in the distributive trade and increased compliance. In the existing State-level VAT structure there are also certain shortcomings as follows. There are, for instance, even now, several taxes which are in the nature of indirect tax on goods and services, such as luxury tax, entertainment tax, etc., and yet not subsumed in the VAT. Moreover, in the present State-level VAT scheme, CENVAT load on the goods remains included in the value of goods to be taxed under State VAT, and contributing to that extent a cascading effect on account of CENVAT element. This CENVAT load needs to be removed. Furthermore, any commodity, in general, is produced on the basis of physical inputs as well as services, and there should be integration of VAT on goods with tax on services at the State level as well, and at the same time there should also be removal of cascading effect of service tax. In the GST, both the cascading effects of CENVAT and service tax are removed with set-off, and a continuous chain of set-off from the original producer's point and service provider's point up to the retailer's level is established which reduces the burden of all cascading effects. This is the essence of GST, and this is why GST is not simply VAT plus service tax but an improvement over the previous system of VAT and disjointed service tax. However, for this GST to be introduced at the Statelevel, it is essential that the States should be given the power of levy of taxation of all services. This power of levy of service taxes has so long been only with the Centre.

A Constitutional Amendment will be made for giving this power also to the States. Moreover, with the introduction of GST, burden of Central Sales Tax (CST) will also be removed. The GST at the State-level is, therefore, justified for (*a*) additional power of levy of taxation of services for the

States; (*b*) system of comprehensive set-off relief, including set-off for cascading burden of CENVAT and service taxes; (*c*) subsuming of several taxes in the GST; and (*d*) removal of burden of CST. Because of the removal of cascading effect, the burden of tax under GST on goods will, in general, fall. The GST at the Central and at the State level will thus give more relief to industry, trade, agriculture and consumers through a more comprehensive and wider coverage of input tax set-off and service tax setoff, subsuming of several taxes in the GST and phasing out of CST. With the GST being properly formulated by appropriate calibration of rates and adequate compensation where necessary, there may also be revenue/ resource gain for both the Centre and the States, primarily through widening of tax base and possibility of a significant improvement in tax-compliance. In other words, the GST may usher in the possibility of a collective gain for industry, trade, agriculture and common consumers as well as for the Central Government and the State Governments. The GST may, indeed, lead to the possibility of collectively positive-sum game.

ADVANTAGES OF IMPLICATION OF GST IN INDIA

The belief that trade and industry will benefit from implementation of GST is widely accepted. Because the GST will give more relief to industry, trade and agriculture through a more comprehensive and wider coverage of input tax set off and service tax in subsuming of several Central and State taxes in the GST and phasing out CST. The transparent and complete chain of set-off which will result in widening of tax base and better tax compliance may also lead to lowering of tax burden on an average dealer in industry, trade and agriculture. It will also boost up economic unification of India and assist in better conformity and revenue resilience; it will evade the cascading effect in Indirect tax regime. In GST system, both Central and state taxes will be collected at the point of sale. Both components (the Central and state GST) will be charged on the manufacturing cost. GST will reduce the tax burden for consumers. It may also broaden the tax base. It will result in cost competitiveness of goods and services in Global market. It will reduce transaction costs for taxpayers through simplified tax compliance. It will result in increased tax collections due to wider tax base and better conformity. It will result in good administration of tax structure. This new tax will also result in a simple, transparent and easy tax structure; merging all levies on goods and services into one GST.

HURDLES IN IMPLEMENTATION OF GST IN INDIA

Bringing about an integration of all taxes levied on goods and services in a federal polity with sharp distribution of legislative power is a herculean task to say the least. The constitution of India 1950 demarcates taxing power in two-tier structure wherein levies on production and international imports are with the Union and post-production levies rest with the states. The centre levies duties of excise on manufactures and import/countervailing duties on international imports apart from levying a tax on services under various taxing entry in the Union list. The state levy VAT on goods sold or entering in the state under various entries of State list. Even if all Union level levies culminate in a single state level levy, this may still have two levies and the resultant cascading and administrative burdens may nevertheless remains to an extent, though this may go a long way in harmonizing levies. A harmonized, integrated and full fledged GST may calls for the following: implementation of GST calls for effecting widespread amendments in the Constitution and the various constitutional entries relating to taxation. Such amendments may virtually transform the Indian federation into an economic Union much along the lines of the European Union. The various levies of the Union and the states are also to be harmonized. In the current scenario it is difficult to visualize constitutional amendments of such far reaching implications going through, more so in view of the fact that sharing of legislative powers is such an essential element of our federal polity and it may be perceived to be a basic feature of the Constitution; services have to be appropriately integrated in the tax network; constitutional amendments required for implementing GST is just one of the major road blocks. No less significant is the issue of an appropriate design and structure of GST. For instance, how the issue of inter-state movement of goods and services may be addressed. The phasing out of CST may go a long way in addressing the issue of inter-state trade and commerce in goods but the crucial issue regarding services originating in one state and being consumed in other state still remains; another contentious issue that is bound to crop up in this regard is the manner of sharing of resources between the Centre and the states and among the states inter se as also the basis of their devolution; apart from all these, there has to be a robust and integrated MIS dedicated to the task of tracking flow of goods and services across the country and rendering accurate accounting of levies associated with such flow of goods and services; and finally, the contentious issue of taxing financial services and e-commerce is to be appropriately addressed and integrated.

RATE STRUCTURE

The Empowered Committee has suggested adopting a two rate structure- a lower rate for necessary items and goods of basic importance and a standard rate for goods in general. There will also be a special rate for precious metals and a list of exempted items. For upholding of special needs of each state as well as a balanced approached to federal flexibility and also for facilitating the introduction of GST, it is being discussed whether the exempted list under VAT regime including goods of local importance may be retained in the exempted list under state GST in the initial years. It is also being suggested whether the Government of India may adapt, to being with a similar approach towards exempted list under The CGST.

The states are of the view that for CGST relating to goods, the Government of India may also have a two-rate structure, with conformity in the levels of rate under the SGST. For taxation of services, there may be a single rate for both CGST and SGST. The exact value of the SGST and CGST rates, including the rate of services, will be made known duly in course of appropriate legislative actions.

INTER-STATE TRANSACTIONS OF GOODS AND SERVICES

Integrated GST (IGST) model for taxation of inter-state transaction of goods and services has been proposed by the discussion paper. According to this model, central would levy IGST which would be CGST plus SGST on all transaction of taxable goods and services with appropriate provision for consignment or stock transfer of goods and services.

The inter-State seller will pay IGST on value addition after adjusting available credit of IGST, CGST, and SGST on his purchases. The Exporting State will transfer to the Centre the credit of SGST used in payment of IGST. The Importing dealer will claim credit of IGST while discharging his output tax liability in his own State. The Centre will transfer to the importing State the credit of IGST used in payment of SGST. The relevant information is also submitted to the Central Agency which will act as a clearing house mechanism, verify the claims and inform the respective governments to transfer the funds. The major advantages of IGST Model are:

(*a*) Maintenance of uninterrupted ITC chain on inter-State transactions;

(*b*) No upfront payment of tax or substantial blockage of funds for the inter-State seller or buyer;

(*c*) No refund claim in exporting State, as ITC is used up while paying the tax;

(*d*) Self monitoring model;

(*e*) Level of computerization is limited to inter-State dealers and Central and State Governments should be able to computerize their processes expeditiously;

(*f*) As all inter-State dealers will be e-registered and correspondence with them will be by e-mail, the compliance level will improve substantially;

(*g*) Model can take 'Business to Business' as well as' Business to Consumer' transactions into account.

Threshold Limits for Levy of GST

Gross Annual Turnover	Central GST	State GST
Goods	INR 15 million	INR 1 million
Services	Yet to be decided; however the threshold may be higher than INR 1 million	INR 1 million

Further a composition/ compounding scheme under State GST (at the option of the tax payer) for tax payers with annual turnover up to INR 5 million has also been proposed. The floor tax rate prescribed for levy of Composition/ Compounding tax is 0.5 per cent across States.

CONCLUSION

Centre opposed the proposed two rated GST model suggested by the Empowered committee and said that the new indirect tax structure should have a single rate as two rates would pose problems. In response to the discussion paper of the empowered committee, the finance ministry held that alcohol and petroleum products should be included in the list of taxable items in the GST regime as against the states' proposal of excluding them. It also recommended a uniform threshold of Rs 10 lakh annual turnover for goods and services for both state GST and Central GST. However, it said the threshold exemption should not apply to dealers and service providers who undertake inter-state supplies.

The Empowered Committee describes the GST as "a further significant improvement—the next logical step—towards a comprehensive indirect tax reforms in the country." Indeed, it has the potential to be the single most important initiative in the fiscal history of India. It can pave the way for modernization of tax administration -make it simpler and more transparent—and significant enhancement in voluntary compliance.

However, these benefits are critically dependent on a neutral and rational design of the GST. The discussion of selected issues in this paper suggests that there are many challenges that lie ahead in such a design. The issues are not trivial or technical. They would require much research and analysis, deft balancing of conflicting interests of various stakeholders, and full political commitment for a fundamental reform of the system.

Opportunities for a fundamental reform present themselves only infrequently, and thus need to be pursued vigorously as and when they do become available. As the choices made today would not be reversible in the near future, one needs a longer-term perspective. Achieving the correct choice is then a political economy balancing act that takes into account the technical options and the differing needs and constraints of the main partners. Fortunately, there is a very substantial consensus among all stakeholders in the country for a genuine reform. In the circumstances, an incremental or timid response would be neither politically expedient, nor would it serve the needs of India of the 21st century. Experience of countries with modern VATs, such as New Zealand, Singapore, and Japan suggests that a GST with single-rate and comprehensive base can be a win-win proposition for taxpayers and the fiscal alike.

7

Conclusion and Suggestions

Service Tax might be internationally recognized in modern times as a new levy and the most prominent revenue earner, but in India it was always there as mentioned in ancient Hindu scriptures. Services rendered as the basis for levying taxes could be traced through *Manusmriti, Sukranitisara, Mahabharata*, and *Kautilya's Arthshastra etc.* In *Mahabharata* taxes considered as the wages of king or his reward for protecting his subjects. Sukra also developed wage theory. He treats king as servant of the people getting his wages in the form of taxes for the protection and growth of his subjects.

In most of the countries where services are taxed selective system of taxing services were adopted. Some of them are Finland, Sweden, Belgium, Netherlands, Germany, New Zealand etc. In almost all the countries personal services like restaurants, entertainment, transport, telecommunication, publicity, repairing services are taxed, professional services of doctors, dentists, teaching services, *etc.* are exempted from taxation. Beside these countries Malaysia, Canada,

Australia, Singapore, USA etc. had also tax on services at different rates.

With the introduction of Globalised policy in the year 1991, Indian economy has moved towards market economy. With this the role of service sector in the economy is increasing very fast and it was found that manufacturing sector is under heavy burden of taxation leaving aside services free from taxes. Therefore, Service Tax was imposed in the year 1994 just after three years of adopting the policy of Globalization. It was imposed on experimental basis and only three services were initially brought under the tax net. When the Service Tax was well placed and the taxpayer in general satisfied with the justification from the new imposition, the Government took the task of expanding the tax base through gradually bringing new services under the tax net.

Another foremost reason for taxing services was widespread corruption in the administration of sales tax. Common people started a strong movement for abolition of sales tax. This development provided the Government with the opportunity to replace sales tax with CENVAT and State VAT and thus its journey towards proposed GST is made very comfortable.

The Chelliah Committee also made specific suggestions about taxation of service sector. It recommended a selective approach covering those services which are in the nature of consumer services as distinct from intermediate producer services so as to avoid cascading effect of tax on tax. In the Budget of 1994-95, three specific services were brought under the tax net, *viz.*, telephones, stockbrokers and non-life insurance services. Thereafter, every year some more services were added in the list of service tax and gradually the number of services on which service tax is imposed have reached 110 within a span of fifteen years. Initially the tax was levied at the rate of 5 per cent and in the year 2003-04 Budget, the rate was raised to 8 per cent and in the Budget of 2005-06 it was raised to 10 per cent. In the year 2006-07

Budget it was raised to 12 per cent. In the interim Budget 2009-10 it is reduced to 10 per cent. Besides this three per cent, educational (two per cent) and secondary and higher education cess (one per cent) has also been imposed on the amount of Service Tax. Thus, the effective Service Tax rate is now 10.30 per cent.

Implementation of economic policies is essentially required to go through the test of constitutionality. At the time of framing the Constitution of India the tax on services was not levied as the role of service sector in the economy was almost negligible. There was no taxing entry authorizing tax on services in either of the List I or II of the Seventh Schedule. Service sector came to lime light only after a shift in the Indian economy from mixed economy to market economy in the year 1991 realizing the great revenue potential from service sector. The Service Tax was imposed in 1994. Initially Service Tax was levied and its constitutional validity was upheld the residuary entry 97. In the year 2003 after the 88th amendment of the Constitution of India the entry 92C taxes on Services were added in the List I of the seventh schedule and Union Government get power to taxes on services. However, the States was not empowered to levy tax on services till date.

The revenue collection from the tax shows steady rise since levied in 1994. The revenue collection was Rs. 410 crores in 1994-95, which increased to Rs. 14196 crores in 2004-05 and shows the average growth of 336.24 per cent. It was further raised to Rs. 23053 in 2005-06, Rs. 38169 in 2006-07, and Rs. 50603 in 2007-08, Rs. 65000 crores in 2008-09 and expected to rise to 68900 in 2009-10. For proper revenue collection of the tax whole country has been divided into 23 zones. Among all the zones Mumbai zone was the major revenue collector zone.

Service Tax is a promising area due to its immense potential as revenue measure the time has now come to shift towards a comprehensive GST with only a few need based exemptions. It is desirable that the rate structure should be confined to only two to three categories. It should be applied uniformly throughout the country as centralized GST enforced on the lines of the existing CST (Central Sales Tax). The present state tax structure should be retained with its confinement of tax on goods only. Presently it is not feasible to give additional power to states to impose Service Tax. However, the full credit of past taxes are to be allowed as credit. If any loss is incurred by the state it should be fully compensated by the central government.

The aforesaid change in the structure of taxes would remove the cascading effect and shall make the whole system transparent. Such a move will boost the tax ratio to GDP and widen the tax base providing the much needed financial succor process of economic growth in India. The proposed GST regime constitutes the next step towards comprehensive reforms of indirect taxes in India. It would be the final step and a step in the right direction. It does seem increasingly a big challenge but it is still a very real and acceptable goal in the eyes of both the Central and State Government circles, regardless of the political persuasion of the parties in power.

The present study initiated on the two hypotheses:

The first being that the indirect taxes continued a lion's share in the Central Government tax kitty, now stands rejected because the picture is fast changing.[1] As we are gradually moving towards developed economy the contribution of direct taxes is bound to get a substantial boost. The proposed introduction of Direct Taxes Code in 2010 is a right step in this direction.

The second hypothesis that Service Tax is assuming an increasingly important role in the indirect taxes of the government is now providing its truth and therefore stands accepted.[2] The reasons are quite evident through the data referred to in the aforesaid study. This stand also gets approval from the fact that the Finance Minister is hopeful of facing the huge revenue deficit out of the expected revenue growth from service sector.

The present work on Service Tax has been divided into seven chapters. The *first chapter* is an 'Introduction' which lays down the perspective in which the role of Service Tax in India has to be studied. The chapter also described the objective, hypotheses, period, purpose of the study and Research Methodology adopted for the present study.

The *second chapter* 'Review of Literature' describes the view of various authors on taxation and indirect taxes in general and specifically on Service Tax. While analyzing the literature on Service Tax it is found that the most of the Litreature is informative in nature. This feature is natural due to short experienced in the functioning of the tax.Various studies on indirect taxes emphasize that indirect taxes play very important role in developing countries as compared to direct taxes. Rao (2001) in his work identify the revenue productivity of taxation of services, rationales for extending the scope of Service Tax net. It also discuss designing and implementing the service taxation and suggests steps to be taken ahead towards adopting a comprehensive approach in taxing services. Available studies describe the need for taxing services in our country, nature and scope of Service Tax and administrative aspects of Service Tax. Krishna (2006) in his study deals with the past and present reform measures and future course of indirect tax reforms. In this work he further deals with the integration of Central Excise and Service Tax and prospects of GST.

The *third chapter* 'Principles of taxation and Historical Perspective' deals with the principle of taxation prevalent in ancient India, Mughal period, the development of taxes during British Rule and after Independence. The Hindu theory of taxation is of immense importance. The various forms of taxes such as *bali, kara, sulka etc.* are found in ancient India. In Mughal period land revenue and *zazia* were the most important direct tax. Zazia was basically a tax on non-Muslims. In British period majority of the present taxes were initiated. Some of these taxes are Income tax in 1860, Excise duty in 1894, Sales tax in 1935, *etc.*. It clearly indicates that the current Indian Tax system is greatly influenced and shaped during the British period.

The *fourth chapter* namely 'A Brief Review of the Tax Structure in India' describes the taxes levied in Independent India. The Constitution of India distributed the taxing power between Union and States. These distributions have been discussed in this chapter. Major direct and indirect taxes are discussed in detail. Indian taxation system suffers from various problems and drawbacks. Therefore, Government has appointed various committees under the chairmanship of different experts. The recommendations of some committees such as Tax Reforms Committee (1991), Task Force on direct and Indirect Taxes (2002) *etc.* have been discussed in this chapter. Beside this revenue receipts from direct and indirect taxes, their contribution in GDP and gross tax revenue has been described in this chapter. The revenue collection from major direct and indirect taxes have also been discussed.

The *fifth chapter* 'Service Tax in India' describes the role of service sector in India. Service sector is being the engine of economic growth since 1990s. Therefore, Finance Minister introduced tax on services by giving emphasis on the importance and growth of this sector in our economy. Legislative history, constitutionality of the tax, justification for imposing Service Tax, Administration, Registration, Exemptions and Challenges, before the revenue department is discussed. Future prospects and the tax feasibility of the proposed GST in India *etc.* is discussed in detail. Initially the tax was levied on three service and year after year services were added in the tax net. Presently, there are 110 taxable services. The revenue collection from the tax shows steady rise. All these aspects of Service Tax have been discussed in this chapter. In this chapter the buoyancy of Service Tax has also been calculated and it is found as the most buoyant tax amongst all the taxes.

The *sixth chapter* 'Revenue contribution of some special services' consist the analysis of 30 specified services. For the purpose of analysis, services are categorized on the basis of their contribution in the total revenue receipts, into three groups, *viz.*, top ten, bottom ten and services with wider scope. Top ten revenue contributor services indicate that these services are having great potentiality from revenue point of view and their contribution is maximum in total revenue receipts. Bottom ten revenue contributor services depict that their collection cost is higher than their contribution. Therefore, these services were either exempted or their administrative efficiency is remained to be further raised. The third group of services include some services with wider scope as future revenue earner. The analysis indicates that, presently these services are not included in top ten but their future prospects are very bright.

The present one is the *last chapter* entitled 'Conclusion and Suggestions'. It consist of the finding and suggestions submitted. In the last not the least this study ends with the concluding remarks.

FINDINGS

The major findings of the research work are as follows:

- After independence indirect taxes were the major revenue contributor in India and it was accounted 56.54 per cent share in total tax revenue of the Central Government.
- In 1950-51 excise duty contributes 50.04 per cent share in the gross tax revenue and corporation tax accounted only 11.59 per cent of gross tax revenue.
- With the introduction of New Economic Policy in 1991 the revenue trend of direct and indirect taxes were changed and the share of direct taxes starts increasing.

- In the year 2008-09 the percentage share in gross tax revenue through corporation tax exceeds over excise duty and it is 32.9 per cent and 20.0 per cent respectively.
- Service Tax has been administered by the Central Board of customs and Excise Department.
- Initially the tax was levied at the rate of 5 per cent later on it was raised to 12 per cent, in the Interim Budget 2009-10 it was revised and reduced to 10 per cent.
- Revenue collection from Service Tax shows rapid increase from Rs 410 crores in 1994-95 to Rs 65000 crores in 2008-09 and expected to rise to Rs 68500 crores in 2009-10.
- The numbers of assessee were increased to 846155 in 2005-06 to 3943 in 1994-95.
- Major revenue contributor services are Telecommunication services, banking and other financial services, Business auxiliary services, stockbroker services, General insurance services, construction services *etc.*
- Telecommunication services alone contribute 18.78 per cent of total tax receipts and stood at 1st position.
- Among bottom ten revenue contributor services we includes opinion poll services, mailing list compilation, survey and map making, underwriter agency services, packing services, cost accountant services *etc.*
- The least revenue contributor service is opinion poll service and it was accounted 0.0034 per cent of total Service Tax collection.
- The other services that are having wider scope from revenue from point of view are advertising agency services, courier services, port services, charted accounted services, cleaning and forwarding agent services, airport services *etc.*

- Among top ten Commissionerate Mumbai service Tax Commissionerate stood at first position and contributes 30.79 per cent of total tax receipts.
- The Buoyancy of the Service Tax with respect to NNP is 3.1358.Which clearly indicates that if there is Re 1 enhancement in NNP that there will be three times increment in Service Tax revenue.
- The Buoyancy of the Service Tax is much more as compared to other taxes. It indicates that the tax is very buoyant as compared to other taxes.
- The Service Tax liability lies on the service provider but ultimately the tax has been paid by the service receiver or the consumer of the service.
- Services are taxed through selective system of tax, which makes the system of tax extremely complex.
- Services like education, health, water supply are contributing significantly towards economic growth therefore; such services are exempted from tax net.
- There are some services which are frequently used by rich and poor both. Some of them are courier, dry cleaning, beauty parlors *etc.* it indicates that the burden is mainly on poor section.
- The tax has been administer and directed by the Custom and Excise department, which makes the law and legislature complex.
- With the expansion of exemption limits up to 10 lakhs so many service providers will go out of the tax net.
- In the year 2010 Goods and Services Tax (GST) will be introduced in India with the integration of Central Excise duty, Sales tax and Service tax.

SUGGESTIONS

- Towards simplification and injecting efficiency on administration of service tax there is need of an independent Service Tax Act.

- There should be separate set up legal authorities for the Service tax.
- Service Tax should be levied in a comprehensive manner leaving out only a few services through them in a negative list.
- Instead of having more than 100 taxable services, it should divide into three or four groups such as Professional services, Utility services, Luxury services *etc.*
- The expansion of service tax area also requires scientific classification & categorization of services so that there is uniformity in its administration all over the country.
- There should be more than one tax rate according to the capacities of service receiver.
- The statutory change towards strengthening of the administrative machinery and effectively prosecutes frequent offenders required special attention.
- Procedural reforms required to be introduced for making it possible to attend to all major court cases relating to Service Tax law for early disposal of cases.
- Deploy adequate staff to attend to service tax work and provide infrastructure and conveyance to implement service tax law effectively.
- Concentration should be put on liquidation of Service Tax arrears and issue necessary clarifications to the field officers so that mounting arrears could be prevented due to disputed interpretations of the provisions of the law.
- Facilitate the implementation of the recommendations of Expert Group set up by the Government, so that steps for early rationalization and enlargement of the scope of service levy in the country are expedited.

- Intensify the field survey operations to ensure that all taxable eligible service tax assesses are brought into the tax net and Service Tax due from them are collected in an efficient manner.
- Some services like underwriter, opinion poll services, survey and map making services *etc.* should be exempted because the revenue contribution of these services are very negligible.
- Legal services and doctor's services should be brought under Service Tax net though a beginning in this direction has already been made in the Finance Act, 2009-10.

CONCLUDING REMARKS

The process of the fiscal economic transformation in India which was initiated with the adoption of Liberalization, Privatization and Globalization is reaching its culmination point. The country is anxiously looking forward to the adoption of the Direct Tax Code and a comprehensive GST.

GST is a new global phenomenon till date it is implemented in about 150 countries. Such a system has many advantages. Its simplification is coupled with efficiency gains which are achieved by integrating all the prevailing central and state indirect taxes. It will make the system transparent, remove the cascading effect, and minimize the scope of tax evasion and avoidance consequently enhancing the public revenue.

The basic framework provided by the Tax Reform Committee (1991) started taking shape with the Finance Act, 1994 introducing tax on only three services. It was just the humble beginning. Gradually the Service Tax net was enlarged to comprehend 110 services during its existence of fifteen years. With the successful implementation of VAT (Value Added Tax) in 2005, the Finance Act, 2006 took the enthusiastic step to declare the strong determination of the country to move towards GST. The Empowered Committee of the State Finance Ministers consensus to adopt dual GST, set up is a landmark in this direction. Though the goal is visible the exact roadmap is still missing. Dual GST is not possible without giving the States, the power to impose Service Tax along with tax on goods. Any such constitutional amendment required 2/3rd majority in the parliament and further required to be approved by 50 per cent of the States. It's a time consuming process and arriving at a consensus is a difficult task. There are several issues yet to be resolved, for example, rate structure, the compensation formula, framing of rules and regulations, training the administrative staff *etc.*

The alternative solution is that as a starting point Central GST should be implemented. The present rules and regulation concerning CST (Central Sales Tax) should be adopted after suitable changes and as regards states the *status quo* should be maintained. The State may be allowed to levy Service Tax on the items enumerated in State List only under State GST.

REFERENCES

1. The percentage share of indirect taxes was 56.54 per cent in 1950-51, 67.37 per cent in 1960- 61, 72.89 per cent in 1970-71, 77.26 per cent in 1980-81, 80.84 per cent in 1990-91, which decreased to 62.9 per cent in 2001-01 and again 44.8 per cent in 2008-09.
2. The Revenue Collection from Service Tax is increased to Rs. 65,000 crores in 2008-09 from Rs. 410 crores in 1994-95.

Bibliography

BOOKS

Aiyangar, K.V. (1965), *Aspect of Ancient Indian Economic Thought*, Banaras Hindu University.

Bagchi, Amaresh and Stern Nicholas (ed.) (1994). *Tax Policy and Planning in Developing Countries*, Oxford University Press, Delhi.

Banerjee, P.N. (1930), *A History of Indian Taxation*, Macmillan & Co., Calcutta. Bangar Yogendra, Bangar Vandana and Sodhani Vineet (2007), *Student's Guide to Indirect Taxes*, Aodhya Prakashan Pvt. Ltd.

Batra, Ashok (2008), *Service Tax: Law and Procedure*, Vol. I & II, Legal Matrix Publication.

Bhargava, R.N. (1954), *Public Finance—Its Theory and Working in India*, Chaitanya Publishing House, Allahabad.

Bhargava, R.N. (1969), *Indian Public Finances*, B.D. Bhargava & Sons, Chandausi.

Bird, Richard and Oliver, Oldman (ed.) (1967), *Readings on Taxation in Developing Countries*, The Johns Hopkins University Press, Baltimore.

Bird, Richard M. and Tantscher Milka Cosanegra De(ed.)(1992), *Improving Tax Administration in Developing Countries*, International Monetary Fund,

Brownlee, O.H. & E.D. Allen (1951), *Economics of Public Finance*, Prentice Hall, New York.

Centre for Monitoring Indian Economy(2006), *Public Finance in India*, CMIE Publication, New Delhi.

Chanda, Rupa. (2002), *Globalization of Services India's Opportunities and Constraints*, Oxford University Press.

Chelliah Raja J. (1971), *Fiscal Policy in Underdeveloped Countries*, Georga Allen and Unwin Ltd.

Chelliah, Raja J. (1999), *Towards Sustainable Growth: Essays in Fiscal and Financial Sector Reforms in India,* Oxford University Press.

Dalton, Hugh. (1945), *Principles of Public Finance,* George Routledged & Sons Ltd., London.

Datey, V.S. (2007), *Indirect Taxes: Law and Practice*, Taxmann Publications Pvt. Ltd., New Delhi.

Datey, V.S. (2008), *Service Tax Ready Reckoner*, Taxman Allied Services Pvt.Ltd.

Devereux, Michael P. (1996), *The Economic of Tax Policy*, Oxford University Press.

Dhingra, Navjot. (2005), Tax *Reforms and Administration,* Deep & Deep Publication, Delhi.

Due, John F. (1963), *Government Finance,* Richard D Irvin, Illinois.

Due, John F.(1970), *Indirect Taxation in Developing Economics*, the John Hopkins Press, Baltimore and London.

Ehtisham, Ahmed & Stern, Nicholas (1991), *The Theory and Practice of Tax Reform*, Cambridge University Press.

Gabhawala, Sunil B. (2006), *Treatise on Service Tax : Law, Practice and Procedure*, Bharat Law House Pvt.Ltd., New Delhi.

Gupta, S.S. (2008), *Taxman's Service Tax: How to Meet Your Obligations*, Vol. I & II, (Taxman Publication Pvt. Ltd.).

Heeller, Peter S. & Rao M. Govinda (ed.) (2006), *Sustainable Fiscal Policy for India : An International Perspective,* Oxford University Press.

Hicks,Ursula (1961), *Public Finance*, Cambridge University Press, Cambrodge.

Hiregange, Madhukar N, Kumar T.R. Rajesh & Sudhir V.S. (2008), *Practical Guide To Service Tax*, Bharat Law House.

Holani, Ravi (2005), *Service Tax: An In Depth Analysis and Scope*, Prakash Publications.

Jain R.K. (2008), *Service Tax Circulars, Clarifications and Notifications 1994 to 2008*, Centax Publication.

Jain, Anil Kumar (2001), *Direct Taxation in India: Some Aspects*, RBSA Publication, Jaipur.

Jain, Inu (1988), *Resource Moblisation and Fiscal Policy*, Deep and Deep Sons, New Delhi.

Jain, Sugan C. and Garg, Rachna (1994), *Taxation and Tax Planning*, Arihant Publishing House, Jaipur.

Jalan, Bimal (1991), *The India Economy: Problems and Prospects*, Penguin India, New Delhi.

James, Simon and Nobes Christopher (1984), *The Economics of Taxation,* Heritage Publishers.

Jha, S.M. (1990), *Taxation and the Indian Economy*, Deep & Deep Publications, New Delhi.

Kane, P.V.(1946), *History of Dharmasastra*, Vol III, Bhandarkar Orient Research Institute, Poona.

Kaur, Harjeet (1990), *Taxation and Development Finance in India*, Classical Publishing Company, New Delhi.

Krishna, V.S. (2006), *Indirect Tax Reforms: Challenge and Response*, Abhinav Publications, New Delhi.

Krishnan, R. & Parthasarthy, R. (2008), *Commercial's Service Tax: One Should Know,* Commercial Law Publication Pvt. Ltd.

Kumar, Dr. Sanjeev. (2007), *Systematic Approach to Indirect Taxes (with Practical Problems & Solutions)*, Bharat Law House Pvt. Ltd., New Delhi.

Lakdawala, D.T. (1956), *Taxation and the Plan*, Popular Book Depot, Bombay.

Lavi R. Mohan.(1997), *Bharat's Service Tax: Concept, Practice and Procedure,* Bharat Law House Pvt.Ltd.

Lavi, R. Mohan & Varadarajan, D. (2002), *Service Tax: Concept, Practice and Procedure,* Bharat Law House Pvt. Ltd, New Delhi.

Lutz, H.L. (1947), *Public Finance*, D. Appleton- Century Company Inc., New York.

Marwah, N. & Pahwa, S.K. (2002), *Service Tax: Law and Procedures*, New Age International Publishers, New Delhi.

Mathew, T. (1975), *Tax Policy: Some Aspect of Theory and Indian Experience*, Kalyani Publishers, Delhi.

Mehta, J.K. (1965), *Public Finance*, Kitab Mahal, Allahabad.

Mukerjee, Suman K. (1994), *Textbook of Economic Development*, Orient Longman.

Parthasathy, C. & Agarwal, Sanjiv(2004), *A Handbook of Service Tax: Law, Practice and Procedure,* Snow White Publication Pvt. Ltd., Mumbai.

Poole, K.E. (1956), *Public Finance and Economic Welfare*, Rinehart, New York.

Prasad, Kunwar Deo (1987), *Taxation in Ancient India*, Mittal Publications, Delhi.

Prest, A.R. (1970), *Public Finance in Theory and Practice*, English Language Book Society and Weidenfeld and Nicholson, London.

Prest, A.R. (1962), *Public Finance in Underdeveloped Countries*, Weidenfeld and Nicholson, London.

Pullani Ravi and Pullani Mahesh. (2008), *Handbook on Service Tax*, Bharat Law House.

Puttawamaiah, K. (ed.) and Swaminathan, M.S. (Foreword) (1994), *Economic Policy and Tax Reform in India,* Indus Publishing Company.

Reddy, P. Veera. ,(2006). *Guide To Service Tax*, Asia Law House.

Ricardo, David.(1962), *Principles of Political Economy and Taxtion*, Everyman's Edition, J.M. Dent and Sons Ltd., London.

Rustagi, T.R.(2002), *Service Tax in India: Law and Practice*, Deeparchie Publication.

Sarangi, Gopinath. (2008-09), *Service Tax Manual*, Centax Publications Pvt. Ltd., New Delhi.

Sarkar, K.R. (1978), *Public Finance in Ancient India*, Abhinav Publications, New Delhi.

Seligman,E.R.A., (1923), *Essays in Taxation*, The Macmillan Co., New York.

Sharma, Sarita and Sharma, N.K. (2001), *Tax Planning*, RBSA Publishers, Jaipur.

Sheth, Mehul. (2008-09), *Service Tax Primer*, Manupatra.

Shome Parthasarthi (2002), *Fiscal Matter*, Oxford

Srivastava, D.K. (2005), *Issues in Indian Public Finance*, New Century Publications, New Delhi.

Subramanian, P.L(2008), *Service Tax Ready Reckoner*, Snow White.

Sury, M.M. (ed.) (2006), *Taxation in India 1925 to 2007: History, Policies, Trends and Outlooks,* New Century Publication, New Delhi.

Sury, M.M,(1997), *The Indian Tax System*, India Tax Institute, Delhi.

Tripathi, R.N. (1968), *Public Finance in Underdeveloped Countries*, World Press, Calcutta.

Vakil, C.N. (1924), *Financial Development in Modern India*, P.S.King & Sons Ltd., London.

JOURNALS

Acharya, Shankar (2005), Thirty Years of Tax Reform in India, *Economic and Political Weekly*, Vol. 40(20).

Agarwal, Pawan (2007), Service Tax on Entertainment and Media Industry, *Service Tax Today*, Vol.9(8), 182-187.

Bagchi, Ameresh (2004), Taxing Services: The Way Forward, *Economic and Political*, Vol. 39(19).

Bhatia, Dr. Sitesh (2005), Service Tax and Its Justification, *Executive Chartered Secretary*, Vol.11(8), 739-740.

Bhowmik, Rita (2000), Role of Service Sector in Indian Economy: An Input-Output Approach, *Artha Vijnana*, Vol.XLII(2), 158-169.

Bokil, Anil., (2003), *Tax Reform in India*, Indian Journal of Commerce, Vol.56(2-3), 95-104.

Chandak, Ashok. (1997), Service Tax: Expanding Revenue Base, *Chartered Accountant*, Vol. 45(11), 46-51.

Chandak, Ashok. (1998), *Service Tax : A Primer for the Accountant*, Vol.47(5), 13-21.

D'Souza, Errol. (2000), What Explains Service Sector Growth?, *Indian Journal of Labour Economics*, Vol.43(4), 829-833.

Das, Gupta (2007), Service Tax—An Overview; *Service Tax Today*, Vol.9(6), 138-142.

Datey, V.S.(1998) , Service Tax; *The Management Accounant*", Vol. 33(12), 931-938.

De, Prithivis K. (2000), Trade in Service: Oppportunities and Constraints, *Yojana*, Vol.44(9), 24-27.

Ghosh, Biswanath and Roy, Arun Kumar.,(1994), Employment Generation in Service Sector, *Southern Economist*, Vol. 33 (7), 9-10.

Jain, Ved.,(2003), Salient Features of Finance Bill 2003 Direct Taxes, *Chartered Accountant*, Vol.51(9), 888-905.

Katti, Prof. Vijaya(1998), Service Sector and Employment, *Yojana*, Vol.42(8), 53-58.

Khadilkar, V.S., (1994), Service Tax, *Excise Law Times*, Vol.72, A84.

Krishnamurthy, H., (1991), Service Sector in the 1990's: Management issues, *Indian Management*, Vol. 30(3), 13-15.

Kumar, M.Satish and Mathur Ashok, (1996), From Tertiary Sector to Services: Some Conceptual Issues and the Indian Seenario, *Indian Journal of Labour Economics*, Vol.39 (1), 33-60.

Madeswaran, S. and Dharmadhikary, Amita. (2000), Income and Employment Growth in Service Sector in India, *Indian Journal of Labour Economics*, Vol.43(4), 835-864.

Malegaon, Suresh S. (2001), The Liberalisation and indirect taxation: An *x*-ray", *Southern Economist*,Vol.39

Mishra, R.N. & Dash, Chinmaya Kumar. (2000), Role of Service Sector in our Economy, *Indian Management*, Vol.39(7), 52-57.

Mittal, J.K. (2001), Widening of Service Tax: Union Budget 2001, *Chartered Secretary*; Vol. XXXI (4).

Mukhopadhyay, Sukumar (2003), Kelkar Committee on Indirect Taxes: A Critique of Final Report", *Economic and Political weekly*, 9-14

Mukhopadhyay, Sukumar., (2003), Indirect Taxes: All relief and no rationalization, *Economic and Political Weekly*, Vol. 38(10), 888-905.

Mukhopadhyay, Sukumar., (2003), Tax Change with Retrospective Effect: A Curious Case, *Economic and Political Weekly*, Vol. 38(16), 1536-1537.

Nathani, Gopal (2007), Rendition of Service from India's *vs.* Services Delivered Outside India, *Service Tax Today*; Vol.7(6),155-158.

Pandey, T.S., (2002), Widening of Tax Base—Issues and Challenges, *Indian Journal of Commerce*, Vol.55(4), 1-11.

Parsuraman, K. (2001), Service Tax: The Tax of the Future, *Chartered Secretary*, Vol. XXI(9), 1043-1046.

Pattabhiraman, V. (2007), Service to Self is Not Liable to Service Tax, *Service Tax Today*, Vol.6 (5),121-123

Ranka, N.M., (2003), Tax Reforms in India, *Journal of Accounting and Finance*, Vol.17(1), 6-13.

Rao, M.Govinda (2001), Taxing Services: Issues and Strategy, *Economic and Political Weekly*, Vol. 24(36), 3999-4006.

Rasure, K.A. (2008), Growing Services Sector Under WTO regime, *Southern Economist*, Vol.46(21) , 15-17.

Rustagi T.R.(1998), Indirect Tax Reforms in Indian Economy, *Vikalpa*, Vol.23(1); 47-59.

Sherry Dr. A.M.(2007), Goods and Service Tax (GST) in India—A Move Towards Tax Reforms, *Service Tax Today*, Vol.7(5), 121-126.

Singh, Bishwa Nath, (2000), Employment generation in India's service sector, *Indian Journal of Labour Economics*, Vol.43 (4), 877-882.

Singh, Pradeep Kumar. (2001), Service Tax: A Tax of Twenty First Century, *Management Accountant*, Vol.36(12), 937-939.

Singhal, P.D. (2004), Service Tax & Classification of Services, *The Management Accountant*, Vol.39 (11). 915-917.

Srivastava B.P.(1995), Service Tax—A Right Step to Broaden the Tax Base, *Excise Law Times*, Vol.78; A41-A43.

Subramanion, P & Raju, G.(2003), Service Tax: A Bird's Eye View, *Southern Economist*, Vol.41(19), 17-18.

Suryanarayanan, S.S., (1995), The Service Sector in India: Structure, Characteristics and Role in Economic Development, *Indian Journal of Labour Economics*, Vol.38(1), 93-99.

Suryanarayanan, S.S., (2000), Service Sector and Employment, *Indian Journal of Labour Economics*, Vol.43(4), 865-875.

Venugopalan, Dr. M.G.(2001), Service Tax: A Tax of the Future, *Chartered Secretary*", Vol.XXI(9), 1038

Verma Anubha(2008), Goods and Service Tax : Eagerly Awaited in India, *Service Tax Today*; Vol.15(3), 44-60

Verma, P.C.,(1997), India's International Trade in Services, *Indian Economic Journal*, Vol.44(3), 103-120.

Vinayagamoorthy, A.(2005), Service Tax Act: Areas Covered in India, *Southern Economist*, Vol.44(6), 13-14.

REPORTS AND GOVERNMENT PUBLICATIONS

Economic Survey, Various issues.

Budget Document, various years.

Indian Public Finance Statistics,Various issues.

RBI Report on Currency and Finance, Various issues.

Report of Expert Group on Service Tax(2000).

Report of Task Force on Direct and Indirect Taxes.(2002).

Report of Tax Reform Committee (1991).

Index